# History and the Media

# History and the Media

Edited by

David Cannadine

First published 2004 by
PALGRAVE MACMILLAN
Houndmills, Basingstoke, Hampshire RG21 6XS and
175 Fifth Avenue, New York, N.Y. 10010
Companies and representatives throughout the world

PALGRAVE MACMILLAN is the global academic imprint of the Palgrave
Macmillan division of St. Martin's Press, LLC and of Palgrave Macmillan Ltd.
Macmillan® is a registered trademark in the United States, United Kingdom
and other countries. Palgrave is a registered trademark in the European
Union and other countries.

ISBN 1–4039–2037–0 hardback

This book is printed on paper suitable for recycling and made from fully
managed and sustained forest sources.

A catalogue record for this book is available from the British Library.

A catalog record for this book is available from the Library of Congress.

10   9   8   7   6   5   4   3   2   1
13   12   11   10   09   08   07   06   05   04

Printed and bound in Great Britain by
Antony Rowe Ltd, Chippenham and Eastbourne

# Contents

# Acknowledgements

Chapter 2 first appeared in *BBC History* and is reproduced by kind permission of BBC History and the author.

Chapter 8 first appeared in the *TLS* and is reproduced by kind permission of the *TLS* and the author.

# Notes on Contributors

**Lord Bragg** is a novelist and broadcaster in television and radio.

**David Cannadine** is Queen Elizabeth the Queen Mother Professor of British History at the Institute of Historical Research, University of London.

**Taylor Downing** is a writer and an independent television producer who has produced more than 200 historical documentaries, including landmark history series, for both British and American television. He is Managing Director of Flashback Television.

**Sir Max Hastings** is a writer and military historian, a former war correspondent and former editor of the *Daily Telegraph* (1986–95).

**Tristram Hunt** is a broadcaster and historian. He lectures at Queen Mary College, University of London.

**Sir Jeremy Isaacs** is a documentary-maker whose work includes: *The World at War, Ireland: A Television History* and *Cold War*. He was founding chief executive of Channel Four (1980–87) and General Director of the Royal Opera House (1988–97).

**Sir Ian Kershaw** is Professor of Modern History at the University of Sheffield.

**Lord Puttnam** is a Labour peer and Oscar-winning producer of films including *Chariots of Fire, The Killing Fields* and *The Mission*.

**Simon Schama**, CBE, is University Professor of Art History and History, Columbia University, and is the author of many books, most recently the three volumes of *A History of Britain*.

**Jean Seaton** is Professor of History at the University of Westminster and the official historian of the British Broadcasting Corporation (BBC).

**Roger Smither** is Keeper of the Film and Video Archive at the Imperial War Museum, London.

**Sir John Tusa** is Managing Director of the Barbican Arts Centre, London, and former Managing Director of the BBC World Service.

# Introduction

In Britain, the late 1990s and early 2000s witnessed what was widely regarded as an unprecedented interest in history: among publishers, in the newspapers, on radio and on film, and (especially) on television; and from the general public who, it seemed, could not get enough of it. Translated into the market-orientated language of our day, it looked as though more history was being produced and consumed than ever before. The reasons for this are neither clear nor consistent (and nor is it yet established whether this was a uniquely British phenomenon). Was it because the advent of New Labour, in May 1997, determined to eradicate much of what they saw as the outmoded and inhibiting past, had the unintended consequence of making that past seem more interesting, immediate and important than hitherto? Was it because the return of Hong Kong to the Chinese in the same year meant the British empire had finally passed into a history that could now be broadly addressed for the first time? Was it because the millennium, the death of the Queen Mother, and the Golden Jubilee of her daughter, prompted unprecedented outbursts of national retrospection? Was it because there are more history graduates in Britain than ever before, with a lifelong passion for the past, who constantly want to read and hear and see more of it? Was it because the time allocated to teaching history in schools was so limited that the media has effectively taken over as the prime educator about the past for the majority of young people? Or was it because the revolution in IT means that more historical information is more easily available to more people than has ever previously been the case?

These questions are easily posed, but have yet to be convincingly answered, and assigned their appropriate (and relative) significance. Moreover, they rest on assumptions which have themselves not yet been tested or proven. How can we truly know whether 'history' is now

1

more 'popular' in Britain than it has ever been in the nation's life? And even if the subject (however defined) is at present unprecedentedly appealing (however measured), we cannot be sure how long this state of affairs will last. Perhaps, in retrospect, the heady excitement of these recent years, just either side of the millennium, will seem more like a blip than a boom. But such hindsight would be at variance with contemporary perceptions. For in our own time, it does indeed seem as though history and the media are more completely interconnected and more variedly intertwined than ever before. But what form – or, more accurately, what forms – does this involvement take? What are the benefits and the possibilities? And what are the dangers and the pitfalls? It was to address these questions that the Institute of Historical Research organised a conference devoted to the subject 'History and the Media', held in London in December 2002. It was attended by four hundred people, some working in the academy, others in the media, and many equally at ease in both worlds; it is in the lectures delivered and sessions held at that conference that most of the following essays originated; and the interleaving, throughout the book, of 'history' chapters and 'media' chapters, reflects the dialogue as it was carried on, back and forth, during those days.

Despite some fears or expectations to the contrary, it was very much a conversation rather than a confrontation, and a mutually rewarding one at that. Of course, in our dichotomy-dominated world, obsessed with such simplistic divides as West–East, black–white, men–women, rich–poor, Christian–Muslim, and so on, it is both tempting and easy to exaggerate the antagonisms between professional historians on the one side, and media people on the other. Here is one such version: academics are reclusive scholars of exemplary integrity, painstakingly uncovering and accumulating knowledge, disinterestedly searching for the truth, and constantly aware of the complexities of the past; while media people, be they newspaper editors, radio and television producers, or Hollywood moguls, have scant regard for evidence or accuracy, want simplified and sensational stories, and are only interested in circulation, audience and profits. Here is another: academics are dry-as-dust Casaubons, self-importantly immersed in their esoteric researches, with no real sense of human reality, public purpose or broader audience; whereas many who work in the media are passionate about the past, know a great deal about it, and care deeply about bringing the best history to the most people. As is invariably the case when complex issues are presented as over-dramatised confrontations, the result is crude and in many ways misleading stereotyping. But like all stereotypes, they also have some basis in fact; and most of them are represented, or alluded to, or hinted at, in the pages which follow.

Yet as is appropriate for the Institute of Historical Research, which has always provided a national forum for discussion and debate about history as both an academic discipline and an essential part of public culture, the purpose of this conference was not so much to promote a confrontation between two separate, monolithic and mutually hostile constituencies, but rather to encourage a conversation between two diverse, engaged and interconnected worlds, which need each other, feed off each other, and have much to learn from each other, to their mutual benefit, and to the public benefit, too. And so, for all the very different perspectives, experiences and opinions that were advanced, described and voiced (and occasionally disputed), it was possible at the end of three days to discern some sort of shared recognition emerging – namely that when it comes to 'doing' history, university academics and media people, and those growing numbers who locate themselves betwixt and between, are engaged in similar and complementary enterprises if not always in shared or identical tasks: grappling with the complexities of evidence, and wondering what to do and what to say when the archives and the sources are simply not there; struggling with the competing claims of narrative and analysis, of telling stories and of explaining change; fretting about word limits, permissions, deadlines and editorial pressures; and worrying about whether the targeted audience will ever be reached or roused. Thus described, doing history in best-selling blockbusters, or in scholarly monographs or in learned articles, is, in its very essence no different from doing history as a thousand-word essay in a newspaper, or as a major series on radio or television, or even as a Hollywood epic.

Of course, it is not always thus. There are some hair-shirted scholars to whom involvement with the media is on principle anathema, selling out and dumbing down; just as there are some television producers who in practice are irresponsible in their use of history – and cavalier in their use of historians. But the participants in the conference, and the contributors to this book, were preponderantly historians who were sympathetic to the possibilities and the problems of the media, and professionals from the media who were sympathetic to the possibilities and the problems of bringing history to it. And it was from this common sense of excitement and concern that a variety of issues were highlighted, and difficulties registered. Most historians think in words: but they are usually many more than newspaper and radio producers require; and for television and film, it is essential that they think primarily in pictures. Yet this is something many academics are unwilling to recognise. A wholly disproportionate amount of television history is about the twentieth century (and thus about the two world wars and the Nazis), but this is partly because public demand remains seemingly insatiable. Yet what about taking a longer or broader view of the past? At its best, television can convey the immediacy of historic events with unrivalled and overpowering vividness; but it is rarely so good in providing context or analysis or perspective or proportion. How can (and should) this be done? And much of the most exciting work being undertaken by historians today tries to present many voices and different viewpoints; but as written and presented, media history is still largely confined to linear narrative. It needs to be more experimental, and to try other modes of exposition and presentation.

These are some of the issues which the following essays help to open up, in the hope that the conversations begun in its pages will be continued, developed and intensified elsewhere. But what is already abundantly clear is that there is now a sufficient body of historical work – in the press, on radio and television, and on film – to justify, make possible and, indeed, demand, a more systematic reflection and analysis than it has so far received, both in the media and by historians. There is a need to stand back, draw breath, take stock – of what has already been done, and of what might be done and should be tried. Nor is that the only manner in which historians could and should be more reflective about their subject on the media, and the media be more reflective about the sorts of history it purveys and promotes. For there are other ways in which their interconnectedness needs thinking about, and even intensifying. Here is one example. Bearing in mind that there is so much history on television, and that there is also so much transmission time being devoted to current affairs, why do these two areas of programming exist in parallel but almost wholly separate worlds? Why is there so rarely an historical input into reporting and interpreting 'the news', which is, after all, itself the first (and sometimes the most influential) version of history? In part, no doubt, the answer is logistical: when major stories break, as they so often do, both rapidly and unexpectedly, there is little likelihood of an expert historian being instantly available to provide the appropriate and necessary perspective. But perhaps there is also a cultural constraint in thinking more broadly about what 'news' really is – namely contemporary history as well as instant journalism.

For while it may be true that there are more media outlets for history than ever before, especially on television, and that this may itself be part of the explanation for the current history boom, it is also important to remember that those many, varied and multiplying outlets are not only purveyors of history: they also have their own histories. And so while, from one perspective, 'history and the media' is about how the latter embraces and projects the former, from another viewpoint it is about how we think about the media historically. Self-evidently, newspapers, radio, television and film are dominated by firms, organisations and institutions which have their own cultures and characteristics, which have existed, developed and changed over time, and which therefore need to be understood historically for broader reasons: for the media has become so all-pervasive a part of twentieth- and twenty-first-century life that the history of the last hundred and more years, and also the history of our own time, is incomplete – indeed, incomprehensible – without it. All of which is simply to repeat that the relationship between 'history' and the 'media' is one of exceptional complexity: as the media publishes and purveys and projects history features, programmes and films of many varied and diverse kinds; as it reports current affairs in ways which will influence both popular perception and historical recollection; and as an important historical phenomenon in its own right, which may in turn influence the sort of history programmes that get commissioned and made.

The essays that follow are by some of the most eminent and experienced practitioners in their chosen fields – historians who not only command the respect of their peers, but who have also worked extensively in the media; and media professionals who often trained as historians, and who are passionate about the subject – and they are by turn informative and provocative, reflective and opinionated, illuminating and suggestive. Unsurprisingly, they do not always agree with each other all of the time: there are debates in this book which, like many other subjects raised less contentiously here, open up territory rather than impose boundaries on it. For helping to sketch out and initiate these conversations, I am deeply grateful to all the speakers and panellists at the original conference; to those many members of the audience who insistently asked questions and put their own points of view; to Taylor Downing for constant help, advice, encouragement and support; and to Geoff Metzger and the History Channel, whose generous sponsorship made the whole enterprise possible. I should also like to record my heartfelt thanks to all the contributors to this book, who without exception produced their essays on time and at the length expected, and to Luciana O'Flaherty and her staff at Palgrave for making this book possible and to Ray Addicott and Chase Publishing Services for seeing the book through the press with such expeditious and expert efficiency.

And finally, I once again set down my indebtedness to my colleague, Dr Debra Birch, who not only organised the original conference, but has also co-ordinated these contributions, with her matchless flair and inimitable good humour. As these acknowledgements make plain, the pleasures and potential of this book lie in the pages that follow. I hope they will be read by anyone who cares about the future of the past, the future of the media, and the future which, together, they will shape and share.

David Cannadine
New Year's Day, 2004
Norfolk

# 1
# Bringing the Past to the Small Screen

*Taylor Downing*

Television history has become very fashionable in recent years. It has been called the 'new rock and roll', the 'new gardening', and even, by Dawn Airey the departing Chief Executive of Channel 5, 'the new sex'. Last week I counted eighteen history programmes in primetime on the five UK terrestrial channels, among them *Timewatch, Secret History, A History of Britain, Lost Worlds, Reputations* and *Time Team* – just some of the series that featured in the last seven days. Then there is The History Channel, broadcasting eighteen hours a day, seven days a week, fifty-two weeks a year. Such has been their success that the BBC launched a rival channel last October, again broadcasting eighteen hours a day using the vast BBC catalogue of history programming made over the last twenty-plus years. In the last week they have been showing *The Face of Tutankhamun, In the Footsteps of Alexander*, and *1914–18*. Broadcasters now talk about the 'three million club' or the 'four million club' as exclusive groups of programme-makers whose history programmes reach this number of viewers. But what does it mean to attract three million viewers week-in, week-out to a historical subject?

\* \* \*

Let me take one example, from my own company Flashback Television. We produce a series called *Battle Stations*, initially made for American television, where it has attracted large audiences to the US History Channel. It is now showing on Channel 4 every Thursday evening at 8.00 p.m. Here is a clip from a programme about the Lancaster bomber, at the beginning of Part 3 of the episode.

Extract from Flashback Television's *Battle Stations* episode 23 'Lancaster Bomber' (2002) includes an interview with veteran Wireless Operator Ginger Stephens. He very humorously describes the bond the members of the crew built up with their aircraft and how for the young fliers, the Lancaster was definitely female. It was always referred to as 'she'.

When this documentary was shown on Channel 4 earlier this year it attracted an audience of 2.6 million – high for the time of evening it was being transmitted, for Channel 4. Late in the afternoon of the day after it was shown we received a call from Ginger Stevens, the interviewee who ended that clip. He had never talked much to family or friends about his days as a Wireless Operator on Lancasters. The post-war questioning about the value of the bombing offensive against Germany had left him feeling unsure about Bomber Command, unhappy about the loss of civilian life in Germany, and, frankly, he felt a little guilty about his part in the war. But fifty-five years after the war he eventually agreed to be interviewed by Flashback to appear in this episode of *Battle Stations*. It was at long last time to 'come out', as he put it to us. During the day after Channel 4 screened this documentary he was stopped repeatedly by total strangers who had seen the programme. As he sat in a traffic jam in his car, a lady in the next vehicle wound her window down and congratulated him on what he had done in the war. Two young black kids sitting opposite him on a train, giggling, asked for his autograph as they had seen him on the television the night before. And a young man came up to him in the street, slapped him on the back and said he wanted to thank him for what he had done to help win the war, and that it was the courage of men like him that had helped to defeat Nazism. All this to a man who for more than half a century had rarely if ever openly talked about his part in the war. Ginger Stephens called the programme's director, Andrew Johnston, and in a state of intense emotion related how he felt he had become like a film star for a day; how a burden had been lifted and how he felt he could now begin to be proud about his role in the war.

\*   \*   \*

This story shows something of how broad and how extensive the audience currently is for history on television. Young and old, male and female, black and white all tune in, in large numbers. Yet like most television, history programmes on the small screen don't have a long ancestry. *The Great War* series produced by the BBC to mark the 50th anniversary of the outbreak of that conflict, in 1964, is usually taken to mark the beginning of the genre. The narration was read with great solemnity by Sir Michael Redgrave. The series had a haunting musical accompaniment, and it was epic in its scope. It was a pioneering example of the effectiveness of combining archive film with eye-witness testimony, and in breaking the history of the war down into bite-sized chunks of narrative which are easily digestible in television time-spans. *The Great War* series was highly dramatic, and it was outstanding television. But it was not always good history, for its use of archive film was dubious to say the least. Feature film footage shot well after the war, often taken in film studios in the 1920s, was freely intercut with authentic record film.

But it was great narrative, and it is narrative that is at the heart of the success of history on television. Let's look at an extract, from Programme 13 called 'The Devil is Coming'. It deals with events on 1 July 1916, the first day of the Battle of the Somme, and was first shown on BBC2 on 20 August 1964:

> Extract from the BBC's *The Great War* episode 13 'The Devil is Coming' (1964) includes both British and German veterans recalling very vividly the horror of the long bombardment preceding the first day of the Battle of the Somme, 1 July 1916.

One of the joys of viewing this series again is the oral history it contains and in seeing the veterans, still looking so young. When they were interviewed by the BBC in the early 1960s, these men were younger than many of the Second World War veterans we see interviewed on our screens today.

*The Great War* series set the style, and to some extent the tone, of history on television, and the BBC thought it had a monopoly in it. Until, nearly ten years after *The Great War*, when Jeremy Isaacs persuaded the Board of Auntie's big commercial rival, Thames Television, to invest in the production of a twenty-six-part series on the history of the Second World War. *The World at War* was three years in the making, and was again epic in scope and content. This time Laurence Olivier read the commentary and Carl Davis wrote the music. Here is an extract from the beginning of Episode 16, 'Inside the Reich', which begins by evoking the mood in Germany after the victories in the summer of 1940.

> Extract from Thames Television's *The World at War* episode 16, 'Inside the Reich' (1974) includes interviews and archive film to evoke the triumphant mood on the home front in Germany in the summer of 1940. It shows soldiers coming home from their victories and being welcomed as heroes.

When *The World at War* was first shown on ITV on Wednesday evenings in 1974, it was an instant success with viewers. It regularly drew audiences of between six and seven million – and some episodes reached twelve million. The critics loved it too and it won an Emmy Award – the Oscar equivalent for television. Not only was *The World at War* a great success at home but Thames International, the selling arm of Thames TV, soon found that it was phenomenally popular around the world. It cleared the rights internationally, and began to sell the series to all the major TV territories. And in the United States, the richest TV market in the world, there have been cable channels that have bought it continuously so that when one run of twenty-six weekly episodes ends, another six-month run begins. For decades now *The World at War* has never been off the television screen in America.

In terms of its content, *The World at War* refined the format created by *The Great War*. To begin with, it was far stricter in its use of archive film. Producers were rigorous about using it correctly, with the same accuracy and objectivity as one would any source material. And those interviewed for the programmes were chosen with great care, to reflect not so much the planning of high strategy and the thoughts of generals (although one or two generals did appear in the series) but rather to illustrate the impact of great events on individuals across the globe. The series was hugely accessible, and not just for those on the winning side of the war. It also sold well in Italy, Germany and Japan. And, more than anything else, *The World at War* was great narrative, and great storytelling.

For many years thereafter, history on television was dominated by two formats. Firstly, there was presenter-led history where the audience was given one, single viewpoint, such as Kenneth Clark on the history of civilisation, or Robert Kee on the history of Ireland. And secondly, there was *The Great War* and *The World at War* format, intercutting eye witness testimony (what we in TV somewhat deprecatingly call 'talking heads') with archive film, using dramatic commentary and powerful music.

\* \* \*

Reliance upon archive film inevitably limited history programmes to subjects for which an ample supply of it existed. Hence there are countless programmes that concentrate on war and conflict – as newsreel cameramen and the military themselves have been busy recording conflict from soon after the emergence of the cinematograph in the mid-1890s. There is competition as to which was the first war to be filmed. The most likely winner seems to be the Spanish–American War of 1898. Certainly by the time of the Boer War there were cameramen like W.K.L. Dickson of the Biograph company filming with the British Army in South Africa. His camera was so huge and bulky it took a team of oxen to drag it along in a cart to somewhere near where the action was taking place. And there were also companies like Mitchell and Kenyon in Blackburn staging events back home for audiences who were eager to follow news of the war in South Africa. From the Spanish–American War, to Afghanistan and Iraq, cameramen have always been near the front line recording and reporting on events that have an obvious historical importance as they happen.

Recently, of course, the appeal of the archive image has been enhanced by the discovery and use of colour footage. Although countless documentaries have used colour footage, this recent revival began with a series on ITV two years ago called *The Second World War in Colour*. The series attracted eight million viewers – an incredible audience for a history programme in today's multi-channel environment. It was followed by *Britain at War in Colour*, *America at War in Colour* and most recently by *The Empire in Colour*. These programmes have exploited the fact that most viewers are accustomed to black and white representations of the past. Without doubt colour gives an immediacy, a 'contemporaryness', a sort of closeness, that black and white does not – especially for younger viewers. These programmes and the scrupulous research that has gone into finding colour images of events that even most *archivists* thought only existed in black and white, have done much to extend the appeal of television history. Alongside the authentic colour footage, for this material was all shot originally in colour, the producers have not used 'talking heads', old men and women recalling events, but they quote from diaries, letters and documents written at the time to give an impression of being present at the events depicted. This makes for compelling television very much in the *present tense*. No octogenarians reminiscing, just the immediacy of colour footage and the freshness of an account written on the day or very soon after an event.

Here is an example from the last series in the genre, *The British Empire in Colour*, shown last September on ITV – an extract from the story of the partition of India and Pakistan in 1947.

Extract from TWI/Carlton Television's *The British Empire in Colour* episode 1 'A Tryst with Destiny' (2002) includes remarkable colour footage of the aftermath of the massacres of Hindus and Moslems along the border following the partition of India and Pakistan.

No one can deny that colour film has an immense impact. The 'problem' with the success of the IN COLOUR brand of programming is that broadcasters now want *everything* in colour. And it won't be long before producers are forced to colourise material to cater for this insatiable demand. Already in production is a First World War series in which the authentic archive film is being colourised. Soon I can imagine the General Strike in colour, the Great Depression in colour, the nationalisation of the coal mines in colour. The technology of colourisation has developed considerably from the days when Ted Turner colourised *Casablanca* – what an absurd idea! – with risible results. The only limitation on colourising material at present is the cost; but once the genie is out of the bottle, and the first colourised series gets audiences of six million, it will never be possible to put it back again. And this will be a very divisive issue because tampering with the historical record will outrage many archivists and purists. Maybe this time next year colourisation will be the big issue facing television history.

But dependence on the moving archival image – whether in black and white or in colour – meant that television history did not for many years address several important subject areas – most obviously social history, diplomatic history, the history of gender, and the relationship between the sexes. In more recent years, however, programme-makers have branched out, with the result that history on television has been substantially and significantly reinvented. Hence *The 1900 House*, *The 1940s House* and *The Edwardian Country House*, all produced by Wall to Wall Television for Channel 4. And hence *The Trench* on the BBC – in which a group of young men were given a taste of what First World War life was like in the front line. These programmes have tried to engage with younger viewers by asking them to imagine themselves transported back in time to a particular historical moment. Interesting and popular though they have been, they usually tell us more about people today than about people's lives sixty, eighty or a hundred years ago. And while *The 1940s House* and *The 1900 House* revealed much about how our grandparents and great grandparents struggled with the realities of everyday life, *The Trench* told us very little about the true horror of warfare on the Western Front. BBC Health and Safety regulations did not permit the firing of live ammunition, the simulation of an artillery bombardment, or the use of mustard gas! This might, by one definition, have been 'reality television'; but it was certainly not 'real history'.

\*   \*   \*

There is another way to bring the past alive and to make it closer to a modern audience – although this has proved unpopular with many historians. During the last three or four years, producers and broadcasters have developed the use of reconstructions to make a point or illustrate a theme. These re-enactments can vary from life in a medieval monastery, to life in the court of Elizabeth I; from a scene in the camp of Napoleon's Army, to a scene at the airfield of an RAF Spitfire squadron during the Battle of Britain. As someone who has been active in this area, I ought to say something about the use of reconstructions in history programmes. For me, historical re-enactments on television are perfectly justifiable when they evoke the spirit of a moment, the detail of a description, or the nature of some machine or piece of technology. They are strong on conveying detail, at creating, if you like, a vignette. They are rarely effective in painting a broad canvas, the scale of a battle, or the mood of a vast crowd. As documentary producers we never have the budgets to spend that Stephen Spielberg and Tom Hanks had on *Band of Brothers*. And it shows. As makers of factual television we will never make combat seem as real as in the wholly dramatised scenes of *Band of Brothers*. How many more times will we see Cromwell winning the battle of Naseby with four lancers and a dozen footsoldiers?

But re-enactments are justifiable in allowing the viewer to see something that a cameraman would have shot had the technology of the time allowed it. So, for instance, in a Second World War programme we see the crew inside a tank or in the cockpit of an aircraft. These spaces were too small and too dark for any 35 mm camera to have operated in at the time with the slow film stock of the 1940s. But they are easily accessible to light sensitive miniature digital cameras today. And more importantly, reconstructions can take us to places that no movie cameras ever went near. They can open up pre-twentieth-century history. And they can reveal elements of twentieth-century history it has been impossible to depict in a visual medium.

Consider the history of espionage. For a medium that can only depict that which has already been shot on film and is now available in the archives, television history could never tell the vital story of espionage or of code breaking for the simple reason that these events were so secret that no one ever filmed them at the time. Even personal photography was strictly banned at Bletchley Park. No newsreel cameras or army film units ever visited the place. But all historians now recognise the crucial part played in the Second World War by the breaking of the German Enigma codes at Bletchley. So programmes about code breaking needed to reconstruct the top secret world of the code breakers. This is what the Channel 4 series called *Station X* did very effectively. It replaced archive film – because none existed – with reconstructions, and placed these alongside the personal testimony of those who were there. This short extract from the first Episode of *Station X* shows how well this can be done:

> Extract from Channel 4's *Station X* (2000) which shows the abandoned offices and corridors of Bletchley Park. The extract goes on to introduce the concept that through interviews and reconstructions the series will recreate the intense wartime activity and the extraordinary work done at the site.

For me, the use of reconstructions has freed up history on television from the tyranny of the archive image. Television can now evoke periods of history outside the twentieth century, and we can explore topics that no one bothered to film or was able to film at the time. And we can convey historical detail in an immediate and relevant way. We cannot reconstruct the past for, by definition, that is over and gone. But we can reconstruct the appearance of the past and include this in our historical narrative. The use of reconstructions has been criticised on the grounds that history is concerned with reality and evidence, whereas reconstructions are about 'pretend' and about fantasy, and are essentially phoney. To be sure, twenty-first-century re-enactors do not look much like, say seventeenth-century people. They are too tall, too healthy and often too heavy. A seventeenth-century citizen was more likely to be disfigured by disease and to have bad teeth. And certainly, reconstructions are not real in the way that a document, a poster, a painting or a photograph are. But as a television producer I operate in a competitive market, and reconstructions do attract viewers, for the very good reason that they bring history alive that would otherwise be dead.

Nevertheless, there must be some rules. Reconstructions should be labelled as such. It might be obvious to anyone who stops to think for a moment that a sequence that shows King Arthur burning the cakes, or Charles II flirting with Nell Gwynne *has* to be a reconstruction. But it might not be so obvious with images purporting to show the captain on the bridge of the Bismarck, or even the assassination of the Archduke Franz Ferdinand. All the programmes I produce label reconstructions quite clearly and I believe all documentaries should do this. And reconstructions are always better when they convey detail – the clothes worn, the interior of a room, the machinery in use in a nineteenth-century iron foundry or a 1940s radar station. But more than anything, reconstructions enable us to make history on television 'in colour'. I've spoken about the insatiable demand for colour images, and I suppose the modest use of reconstructions is a way of complementing this. Of course, it's not real. Of course, it can be overdone. Of course, baggy tights and historical anomalies can be absurd. But when done well, the reconstruction can take the viewer into the tortured soul of Mary Queen of Scots, or inside a Lancaster bomber once it has been hit and the crew are struggling with the controls to return home. And it is history in colour not just in the sense of colour against black and white, but in the sense of colour helping to make an event seem closer, helping to create a sense of being there and of being able to excite the imagination. History for me has always been in colour.

*   *   *

There is another type of television history that used to be popular, then became unfashionable and now has returned to our screens, and that is presenter-led programmes. During the 1960s A.J.P. Taylor delivered his lectures straight to camera and captivated many more than mere history undergraduates. I doubt this would work today, no matter how compelling the lecturer. Now we have Richard Holmes striding across the battlefield, David Starkey guiding us down the corridors of Tudor England, and Simon Schama navigating us across the choppy ocean of British history. These historians are amongst the best-paid presenters on British television, and I'm sure their success will have won them many enemies in the Senior Common Room. But from the perspective of history on television they are doing a magnificent job. They have attracted millions of viewers to history who have never picked up an academic history book. They have captured the imaginations of those who rarely visit a historical site. They have encouraged millions to think about the shape of the past and how we come to be what we are today.

Here is an example from Episode 11 of Simon Schama's *A History of Britain* about the horrors of slavery:

> Extract from BBC TV's *A History of Britain* episode 11 'The Wrong Empire' (2001) in which powerful graphics, music and location filming including images of chained feet walking along a beach combine with Simon Schama's dramatic narrative to evoke the horrors of the African slave trade. Schama's piece to camera is delivered whilst handling and then describing a branding iron.

As this clip vividly demonstrates, a good history presenter takes the viewer through a slice of the past, by giving his own perspective on it.

But all historians do that, all the time. The presenter can be shot in a real location, at the scene of an event, which sometimes can be visually dramatic, although often it is not. Many a time I've struggled to make a flat, windswept turnip field look 'historic'. 'But this is where it actually happened' someone cries. Location shooting can be supplemented, as is often the case with David Starkey and Simon Schama, with imaginatively created reconstructions. But in the end it is down to the narrative that the presenter tells. The Holmeses, Starkeys and Schamas are the storytellers of our age. They are the ones who bring the research out of the academy and offer it to the many.

In the past, presenters have traditionally been male. And inevitably, they have brought a male perspective on the past – although Schama's history of late eighteenth- and nineteenth-century Britain was at pains to include the experience of women. But on Channel 4, Bettany Hughes has recently been presenting the history of the Spartans. You might have thought there would never be a *more* male-oriented subject than the history of Sparta with its slavish and sweaty world of male warriors trained from an early age for the glory of combat. But Hughes brought a distinctive viewpoint that probably many male presenters would have missed, as should be clear from this extract about Spartan women:

> Extract from Channel 4's *Sparta* (2002) in which Bettany Hughes points out that women were involved in every part of the rituals that surrounded their brothers, fathers or husbands in ancient Sparta. On location and in an exhibition hall she explores the often sexually charged role of Spartan women.

\* \* \*

There is a variety of ways in which television historians, like myself, can relate to or provide a link with the Academy, with professional historians, primarily in the universities but also including that broader constituency of archivists, curators and those who earn their living from the research and study of history. For instance, the teams of programme-makers whom I produce rarely have time to do original research – except in the field of oral history. We are reliant upon the work that has been and is being done by scholars and researchers around the world. I believe passionately that part of what television history should be doing is providing a bridge between the academy and the mass television audience. We should be helping to bring some of the new understandings, the new insights, the new interpretations, the new narratives, that professional historians are working on, into the public domain, where they can be taken in and debated by millions of people. Good television history should be placing the latest understanding of the past in front of a bigger constituency than those who habitually read history books.

Here is one example. During the late 1990s, I worked on a series made for American television, but also here shown on BBC2, called *Cold War*. The twenty-four one-hour programmes were made seven or eight years after the Berlin Wall had come down, the Iron Curtain had gone up, and the archives of what used to be called the Communist bloc had begun to open. We were determined that this series should bring some of the new understandings of what had really gone on during the sometimes frightening days of the Cold War to as large an audience as possible. One of our principal advisory bodies was the Cold War International History Project based in Washington. It publishes a *Bulletin*, with translations of vast numbers of documents trawled from archives in Moscow, Beijing, Eastern Europe, Africa and Asia. Another advisory body to the series was the National Security Archive in Washington whose staff are constantly obtaining access and making available to scholars documents from the US federal archives. All these documents are helping historians to rewrite the history of the Cold War.

But the *Bulletin* is seen by at best a few thousand readers, while a new book on the Cuban missile crisis, or on the causes of the Korean War, or on Soviet relations with their Eastern European satellites, might be read by some tens of thousands. In the *Cold War* series we were relying on this new scholarship but wanted to try to get it across to a large, thinking public who would be unlikely to pick up a history book and who would certainly never read a seven-hundred-page Bulletin of the Cold War International History Project. We wanted viewers whom we hoped would be attracted to a popular TV series to pick up on and to understand some of the new narratives of the past that were emerging from the archives but were still not widely reported. Professor John Gaddis was one of our consultants on the series, and he was deeply committed to getting these new interpretations, these new narratives of the Cold War, out to the broadest possible audience.

Television historians should at their best be popular historians translating some of this work into narratives that will appeal to the many millions of intelligent viewers who don't want to spend their valuable leisure time in front of *Who Wants to be a Millionaire*, or *The Weakest Link*, or watching another episode of *EastEnders*. For there are millions of intelligent and thinking people who are genuinely interested in how the past has helped to make us what we are. And of all the letters that I receive after a TV programme has been broadcast, none is more satisfying than the letters that say 'I hated history at school but I was really fascinated by this programme on...'. Someone who never used to go near a history book has been won over and their imagination has been excited by the past.

Here is a final extract, from *Cold War* Episode 8, 'Sputnik'. Well known throughout the Cold War are the moments of intense tension between the West and the Soviet bloc – Berlin, Cuba, the Yom Kippur War. Less well known are the accidents that threatened nuclear catastrophe. This clip records an accident inside the Soviet Union that was kept totally secret until the 1990s; and also the argument about the 'missile gap' inherited by Kennedy:

> Extract from Jeremy Isaacs Production's *Cold War* episode 8 'Sputnik' (1996) which shows film not seen before in the West of a terrible missile accident in the Soviet Union in which hundreds of scientists were killed. Robert McNamara then goes on to admit that in 1961 when Kennedy became President the missile 'gap' was in favour of the US not against it.

\* \* \*

I hope that the relationship between television history and the professional history of the academic, the curator and the archivist is not just a one-way process in which television history takes from and popularises the work of the 'serious historian'. I hope that television history acts as a sort of shop window for the broad community of history, promoting interest amongst the general public in history, helping academics make the case for public funding, and driving visitors to castles, country houses and heritage sites. I know that the long-running series *Time Team* is thought to be behind the large increase in applications for undergraduate places on Archaeology courses, and it seems to me that every Waterstones or Borders today has many more history books on display than it used to. I would like to think that all this is at least in part linked to the millions watching television history. But maybe there is simply a broad appetite for the past in early twenty-first-century society and television history along with the popularity of historical books, the numbers of re-enactment events that take place around the country, and the huge interest in genealogy are all symptoms of this.

I have been trying to argue that history on television today covers a multitude of different styles, formats and techniques, and that that is one of the reasons why it is so popular. But all successful television history programmes share one or two essential characteristics. Firstly, television is a visual medium: I earn my living by finding visually compelling ways to express ideas, which means I need a strong visual core to my programmes. It can come from archive film or photographs, it can come from people recalling events, it can come from reconstructions, it can come from a talented expert capable of telling stories well. But equally important, it must be good *narrative*. Many historians might part company here, saying that history is not about narrative, it is about evaluation, it is about evidence, it is about interpretation. But from Herodotus onwards history has always been about storytelling, and that the best historians have always been those who can communicate well, not just with other historians but with the broader community around them.

A few years ago, I might have been embarrassed to stand up and say that I regard myself as a storyteller. But not any more. Robert McCrum in the *Observer* reassured us recently that 'Narrative is back in fashion', and that 'From the caves of Lascaux to the next Harry Potter, man has been a story telling animal. Narrative is part of our DNA.' Making history on television is about understanding the strengths of the TV medium – its visual foundation, the power of storytelling, the ability to get information across to millions of interested viewers. The opportunity, I hope, of being able to contribute towards the making of an intelligent, informed and sane society. Of course, the medium also has its weaknesses – the baggy tights; the hurriedly written and incorrect commentary – there's *never* enough time; the cliché, visual and verbal; the obsession with war. But throughout my professional career I have always been concerned with the best, and I fervently believe that historians from the academy, from museums and from the archives, should collaborate and work together with television producers to reach the vast numbers who want to be stimulated and provoked by what they watch on the small screen.

# 2
# Television and the Trouble with History

*Simon Schama*

It could, of course, have been the other way round, couldn't it: 'History and the Trouble with Television'? The usual moan of the Common Room and the opinion columns that 'serious television' (in the words of Neil Postman's polemic, *Amusing Ourselves to Death*) is a 'contradiction in terms'; that the subtlety of history is too elusive, too fine and slippery to be caught in television's big, hammy fist; that try as it might, television can't help but simplify the complications; personalise the abstract; sentimentalise the ideological and just forget about the deep structures – all of which are assumed to be at the heart of what my colleagues (on that side of the fence) like to call real history. Which always puts me in mind of another aside overheard by its target: 'oh he's not really a historian, he's a writer'. Which makes me, I suppose, doubly unreal; being not just a writer but a television presenter, I want to try and refute all of the above prejudices. You didn't seriously expect me to promote the usual dialogue of the deaf whereby scholars berate the vulgarity of the medium for failing to understand the nature of historical debates, and producers return the compliment by charging that print historians are no more capable of telling stories in images than they are cooking a souffle or changing a tyre (probably less).

What we – and from the beginning it's really been a collective enterprise – have tried to make of *A History of Britain* has been a project that would make those ingrained prejudices a thing, if you'll excuse the phrase, of the past. Our producers have all been, in whatever terms you want to cast it, real historians, and I certainly hope that they think their writer and presenter has become at least in working outline form, a filmmaker. Which is not to say it's always been easy. There were times, especially shooting in the far west of Ireland in February, or in Skara Brae in July in what seemed to be light sleet, or in Jura in December, when I've prayed for the intervention of the Angel of History. What's more I'd know him when I saw him because Walter Benjamin, the German-Jewish critic, described what he looked like in one of his 'Theses on the Philosophy of History' (don't worry they're only a paragraph long); the last thing he wrote in 1940 before his suicide. This *Angelus Novus*, the new angel, was what Paul Klee called the figure he'd painted as a watercolour, a picture Benjamin had owned since 1921. The angel eyes, Benjamin wrote

> are staring; his mouth is open, his wings are spread. His face is turned toward the past. Where we perceive a chain of events, he sees one single catastrophe which keeps piling wreckage upon wreckage and hurls it at his feet. The angel would like to stay, to awaken the dead and make whole what has been smashed. But a storm is blowing from Paradise. It has got caught in his wings with such violence that he cannot close them. The storm blows him irresistibly into the future on which he has turned his back, while the pile of debris mounts to the skies.

*   *   *

Not much help, then, to be expected from this angel after all; a decidedly weak and wasted creature; less the master than the victim of history; the demoralised opposite of the 'real' historian's presumption that he can order the chaos; make whole the fragments; make sense of the mess; impose music on the cacophony. But then, of course, this was Benjamin's point; this indeed was why he projected on to Klee's painting, a self-portrait of the thinker on the verge of paralysed despair, thunderstruck by a vision of disasters he had been impotent to set right and a calamity to which he was being helplessly pushed; in Benjamin's case, backwards right off the cliff. For, in September 1940, denied the exit visa to make the crossing from Vichy France to Spain, Benjamin killed himself.

There are calamities and then there are mere predicaments. Does that description – the unnaturally staring eyes; the always open mouth; the pointlessly gesticulating arms; the pose which pretends to poise but which actually often verges on controlled panic – remind you of anyone? Are there any other writer-presenters out there? Not to make light of Benjamin's predicament, but you know the feeling; never quite having the luxury of enough time (especially edit time) to be able to consider the careful thought; to give utterance to the finely tuned epigram that happens to be true as well as stylish. Why? Because of the law of the 57-minute programme. And because a storm is blowing in from

Paradise, otherwise known as the Channel Controller's office, which pushes us into the future to which our back is turned – the next schedule; the next budget round; the next seasonal schedule; the next way to be one-up on the opposition.

On the other hand, it would be a bit rich or, as we say on this side of the pond, unseemly, for someone who was, in the end, given four whole years to complete our fifteen programmes, to whine about this. Graduate students are always making the same complaint; and the longer they are allowed extensions, the longer they say they need – until some magical moment of critical mass is reached when they know they have arrived at the definitive truth. This is the scholar's mirage, certain to disappear the closer one approaches it. So the line between invigorating urgency and panic-stricken haste – the line all of us in television choose to live with – is often very fine.

For that matter, Benjamin should not be read as someone who pined nostalgically for the leisurely coherence of the old master texts of history. Just the reverse in fact. For good or ill, the chopped-up, speed-driven, flickeringly restless quality of modern communication, he thought, was here to stay. It was the way the mass of people led their lives. They received information serially, in columns not pages; their picture of the world was scrambled; cubist not classical (look at *Guernica*); rhetoric passed through fields of sonic distortion; topography (we might add since Benjamin, predictably, was neither much of a walker nor driver) glimpsed through the flickering flash of car-windows; each one the equivalent of a celluloid frame.

Now all this might be regrettable, but there it was. If writers whose vocation was the moral rescue of humanity turned their backs on it, then they also turned their backs on modern life. They became mere Brahmins closeted with their refinement, incapable of anything except the mutual exchange of muttered regrets and lamentations. And that would leave the field to the manipulators, whether in the tabloids or the film studios; the likes of Leni Riefenstahl, German film-maker of the Nazi era, and Mosfilm, the Soviet movie company. It was precisely at moments of danger Benjamin thought – and so do I – that history's call to capture memory was itself most pressing. For, not to put too fine a point on it, on that 'capture' by the good guys (as distinct, say, from Al Jazeera) depend all the ancient causes for which the keepers of memory – us – have staked something ultimately more important than faculty tenure – freedom, empathy, community.

Big words, I know; the kind of words to which most self-described professional historians, in this country at any rate, are famously allergic;

the logo on their tunics that of the Nike empiricist: 'Just Do It' (or in academic speak 'Just Get On With It'). But the 'It' that is being got on with (if got on with properly) is, even inadvertently, the carrier of these big things. History, the repository of shared memory, as Orwell insisted in *1984*, was, necessarily, the enemy of determinist inevitability. Because in its texts lay pictures of alternative worlds; the buds of different outcomes. It would have to be critical history to be sure, not the kind manipulated for self-reinforcement. Which is why theocracies and tyrannies can never live with it. Second big word: empathy, if you like, 'alterity', immersion into the experience of others separated from us in time. Without the willingness to reach towards their world, their mental habits, history just becomes, once again, an exercise in self-admiration; exactly the kind of history those theocracies and tyrannies like to teach. Third big word: community, or less sententiously if you like: connection; negatively expressed, the demystification of perpetual difference. The Vikings were always the enemies of the English? No, the Vikings *were* the English. Once too there was a history shared by Muslims and Jews, by Muslims and Hindus; by the English and the Scots; there once was even a time (though admittedly lost in the mists of antiquity) when there was a Conservative majority in the House of Commons.

* * *

If you accept the premise that, as Benjamin wanted, in a time of danger history needs to capture memory (before the bad guys hold it hostage), can television, must television ride to the rescue? Should it set its sights higher than low-budget costume shows, nostalgia-fixes, tonics for the patriotically insecure who want to pull the covers over their heads and be sent to sleep by Tudor lullabies and wake up perhaps with a strange urge, if not to go around executing enemies, then at least issuing Parliamentary Acts in Restraint of the Euro: 'England is an empire, entire of itself'? Now that it does seem to have a mass audience, can television history get serious without breaking the spell?

The answer from some (not all) quarters of the academy has been 'of course not'; because of all the reasons I listed at the beginning. The verdict is based on four interconnected assumptions all of which you'll be happy to hear, are mistakes. The first is that real history is essentially coterminous with the printed book; the second is that only printed text is capable of carrying serious argument, compared to which images, still or moving, are necessarily weak carriers of meaning and debate, essentially auxiliary and this expendably frivolous illustration. Thirdly;

that, for all the flirtation of scholars with writing for popular readership, history remains shaped by full-time professionals, hewers at the rock-face of the archives who alone have the esoteric knowledge (the 'training' as academia likes to say) to define both the terms of the debates and just who is allowed to join them. Consequently, and finally, the success of television history is judged (just take a look at academic written reviews of *A History of Britain* in *History Today* for example) by the degree to which the preoccupations of print historians are faithfully translated and reproduced on television.

So let me just clear the decks before I say something positive about what we can do and how we do it. First, history, even Western history, has not been purely coeval with the printed text. If the scholars of the change from oral to written history – such as the late Eric Havelock at Yale – have taught us anything, it's that the beginnings of Western history were meant, especially in the hands of Herodotus, as part of the oral, and performative tradition. Beyond the monk-written memorials and muniments, there remained of course a strong, unofficial tradition of performative history; strongest indeed exactly where it reached beyond a small cluster of brethren. So, whether he knew it or not, and I strongly suspect he did, A.J.P. Taylor, the grand-daddy of all television historians, was reviving that tradition as has been the great oral Chicago historian, Studs Terkel, dean not of a faculty, but of radio history in the USA.

Second: the triple mistake that print is deep, images are shallow; that print actively argues and images passively illustrate. Now this particular blunder is a result, I suppose, of the self-reinforcing failure of all those graduate departments to educate their students in iconography (the scholarship of the meaning of images) and iconology (the relationship of those meanings to the cultures which produce and receive them). 'Don't know' is echoed by 'don't need to know'. The prejudice born of this visual philistinism is that images are somehow a product or obedient expression of the things that historians habitually do know about: political power; economics; religious doctrine. But images can constitute culture as well as be constituted by it. The regime which, in effect, killed Benjamin was a prime case in point of empowerment through spectacle, as Albert Speer, the impresario of Hitler's 'cathedral of light' at Nuremberg and Riefenstahl who filmed it for mass diffusion, both well knew.

\*   \*   \*

All we have to do is to look up at the Banqueting House ceiling to Rubens's paintings to see how the unreadable fantasies of James I concerning the godlike powers of the monarch, once translated into celestial imagery, could become persuasively spellbinding. What better place to show the apotheosis of the king – literally a translation into a deity, akin to, say becoming Director General of the BBC – than above our heads? And since the paintings were commissioned by his son Charles I, they embody filial devotion too, and (in the near painting) the union, in the Stuarts, of the English and Scottish crowns. It was just because this Great Britain was a marriage made only in the heavenly sphere of the ceiling painter that, once brought down to earth, it created, in effect, the Civil War; a war which among other things was a conflict between *logos* and *icon*, word and image.

There's another example, drawn from our Programme 14, 'The Empire of Good Intentions', of the ways in which images make history as much as they are made by it: two very different uses of the Victorian camera; one to show what David Cannadine has called the 'ornamentalism' of the British empire – hence the match between the romantic-exotic Viceroy, Lytton and the self-conscious parade of Indian 'feudal' princes; the other camera to record, as you'll see a very different but absolutely contemporary India. One set of photographs, playing to neo-feudal fantasies of the exotic, displaying bejewelled and extravagantly moustachioed maharajahs, became popular. Not surprisingly, the other set, of famine victims, reduced almost to living carrion and taken by appalled missionaries, using newly portable Kodak One cameras, did not.

\* \* \*

Imagery, still or moving, does not just tell stories. It argues; but it argues in a different way in print, and it ought to be the first rule for television historians to embrace that difference. Non-fiction writing need not be absolutely linear. Because of the permanent, simultaneous way in which highly diverse details can be carried within the same book, it is possible to jump back and forth between sections – even at the cost of abandoning the cumulative engagement that comes from the pleasure of following rich narrative. In Norman Davies' *The Isles*, for instance, a work that argues against any sort of coherent experience, for something he thinks is the spurious and short-lived invention 'Britain', the broken form of the book itself actually mimics or acts out Davies' argument, balkanising the story into a multitude of parts, held together only by loose chronology. This process of textual atomisation is, like the argument, arbitrarily stopped at the point at which nations deemed 'authentic' – Scotland, Wales and Ireland – are allowed to retain their coherence, even though the history of those entities is one of endless, centrifugal conflict between regions and religions, and is open to precisely the same objection of arbitrary state-building as Davies' 'inauthentic' Britain.

But, even supposing I believed that a series on British history should be boiled down to its bedrock nations (which I don't), it would be impossible to produce a series in which each of the programmes devoted a token number of minutes, in ethnically correct proportion, to a population, and still sustain a coherent, let alone engaging, narrative. So while we (that is the Scottish–Jewish Martin Davidson–Simon Schama producer–presenter partnership) have been accused of being thoughtlessly Anglocentric, the opposite was the case. Committed to the issue, we took a conscious decision that, rather than break up each and every programme, we would spend entire programmes on precisely the 'British nations problem'. As a result, 'Nations' (*A History of Britain*: Episode 4) is about the imperialism of the Plantagenet monarchy in Wales and Scotland (and the imperialism of the Bruce family in Ireland). 'The British Wars' (Episode 8) locates the initiation of the British civil wars in Scotland and Ireland; 'Britannia Incorporated' (Episode 10) is about the eighteenth-century transformation of Scotland, and 'Empire of Good Intentions' (Episode 14) sets the Irish and Indian famines of the nineteenth century side by side.

We also knew that we needed to find visually economic ways of making our points. Here is one of them: our Culloden. As Peter Watkins's great 1960s television documentary *Culloden* made obvious – itself a turning point in historical film-making – there are all sorts of brutally shocking things about that hour-long slaughter. We didn't want to compete with their graphic battlefield carnage; but we *did* want to shock. So we used the history of music, one very familiar piece (the additional triumphalist verse written to 'God Save the King') to make our point.

\* \* \*

It has also been said, and lazily repeated by both academic and journalist critics, that the series has been 'all kings and queens' – in which case they must have been looking at some other series. We make no apology for medieval programmes that concentrated, for example, on the nature of kingship and the constraints on its authority, by looking at the Angevins – Henry II, Richard and John. Any programme purporting to deal with medieval England which did not do that, or a programme about the Norman Conquest that reduced Hastings to a fly-by footnote, would be perverse. In other programmes, even in medieval programmes where monarchs were indisputably history-makers, we endeavoured to put the kings, as it were, in their historical place. The story of Richard II, for example, emerges out of a picture of a world traumatised by the Black Death and in the context of the Peasants' Revolt.

It is sometimes the same historians who have argued that there was nothing intrinsic in the state of the Roman Church in England that would have brought down the Reformation upon it, had Henry VIII not been in desperate need of a male heir (and who presumably, therefore, see Tudor state policy as the motor of change). They have also criticised us for being over-preoccupied with the royal divorce and the relationship between Henry and Anne Boleyn. What, in the scholarly world passes as thoughtful revision, becomes, when turned into television, 'soap opera'.

Underlying many of these complaints is a deep-rooted prejudice against the possibility of serious television history, given that the subject is held to be too important to be left to bungling (as it is implied) 'amateurs'. 'Real' history is, apparently, the monopoly of the academy. Whenever something like this is said, it reminds me of the great medievalist Oxford professor, Bishop Stubbs who, in his inaugural lecture, warned that it would be a waste of time and effort, perhaps a dangerous waste of time and effort, to teach history in the schools. He was, of course, thinking only of boys' schools. Girls, it is safe to say, seldom entered the episcopal-pedagogic mind. For Stubbs and his generation, the integrity of historical scholarship was conditional on its separation from the contamination of the vulgar world. So the walls and archives were to be raised in its colleges, behind which the priesthood could pursue its disinterested research far from the clamour. But, of course, the research was never purely disinterested and what the walls came to shelter was an enormously ramified profession, institutionalised through the triple initiation rites of tutorial essay, examinations and lectures, whose first obligation, as the late French sociologist Pierre Bourdieu pointed out with unkind candour, was its own collective self-reproduction.

Now those walls have been overthrown and television history especially – I'm proud to say – has been part of the demolition squad. Public access to the digital archive is stripping away that particular mystique. In some of the pioneering efforts, such as the Library of Congress's *American Memories* site, where primary sources, textual, visual and oral, are made available at every level of enquiry, from the highest of high scholars, to casual browsers and family researchers, the usual hierarchies of authority have been turned at last into something approaching a democracy of knowledge. At Edward Ayres' extraordinary Civil War website at the University of Virginia, students of all ages, whether at high school, on PhD programmes or adult learning courses, are able to browse archival materials, exchange research data and written essays, and share a multitude of sources – from Confederate and Union army records and slave songs, private diaries and correspondence to the photo-archives of the counties of Pennsylvania and Virginia directly affected by the conflict. In place of a profession, we now, at last, have the real possibility of a community.

*   *   *

This is, I know, all very high-minded. But none of it will work – especially not what I obstinately believe to be 'serious television' – if we uncouple storytelling from argument and debate. Now it is the anti-televisual lobby's point that these functions are incompatible. Even Macaulay who, in a famous 1825 book review of Hallam's *Constitutional History of England*, first insisted that history was divided into two realms, that of poetry and that of philosophy, believed no one had ever managed to bring the two together. He also believed, however, that it was every historian's duty to try. If we substitute narrative and debate for those divisional headings, then it seems also true, even in television, that we too often segregate them. Debate belongs to *Newsnight* and to *Question Time* – 'Now Mr Cromwell, or "Protector" as you seem, for some reason, to think of yourself, I PUT IT TO YOU, that you behaved very, VERY badly in Ireland. No, no, I won't take ifs and buts. Did you or did you not say these RUDE things about the Catholics, and are these the kind of things likely to bring about the "healing" you seem to be going on about much of the time. YES OR NO?'

The closest, in fact, that compelling historical reconstruction has come to embodying the prime time manners of contemporary news debate was the original *Culloden*, which used the device of a war correspondent in eighteenth-century costume, reporting from behind a wall, along with hard-bitten, capsule biographies of the soldiers, British and Jacobite, in the manner of fly-on-the-moor reality reporting. Some of this hasn't, in my view, stood the test of time very well although the parade of grimy faces (and authentically terrible teeth) in *Culloden* succeeded brilliantly in de-romanticising the rebellion – a misery without heroes or villains, just pawns and aristocrats. And the pre-Python danger of a parody of 1960s-style investigative documentaries ('Angus Macdonald, 31; shepherd; conscripted by his tacksman to join the Prince!') disappears altogether in the utterly convincing battle sequences, that were edited virtually to real time (since *Culloden* lasted barely more than an hour).

Those sequences were some of the bravest and earliest experiments in what I want to call 'the poetics of television history'. What that calls for is the sense of surrounding the viewer, for at least some moments, in a different world; and (even harder) making the viewer forget for those same moments that the outcome of that history is already known. What we might call 'historical reality' series (were that not an oxymoron) – *The 1900 House, The Edwardian Country House, The Trench* – sometimes seem as though they are in that same enterprise, but actually they're not, since our involvement with the characters depends on us knowing that they are really 'like us', or that, in so far as they can be made unlike us, the agency of that transformation is social and material – washing with lye, tying a corset. To truly complete the change, the washing, I think, has to be mental or imaginative, as much as physical. Poetic reconstruction, if it is to work, needs to lose the characters, and by extension, us, who are watching them, entirely within their own world without any inkling of their return trip to the contemporary.

*   *   *

Now this is an unbelievably difficult feat to bring off. Those of us who choose to do it are attempting, in effect, to create a drama; to deliver the immediacy of a past world, but do it on a documentary budget and usually, these days, in the unforgivingly crisply focused medium of tape. The ritual complaints – and many of them aren't necessarily wrong – about the clumsiness or the self-consciousness of reconstructions, come from a culture where the standards are set by drama (such as Peter Ackroyd's recent *Dickens* series) funded to supply hordes of extras, wardrobe and make-up on location, professionally dressed sets, professional actors and – most importantly – shot on film.

Having heard both sides of the eternal tape-versus-film debate, and having had to work with both (and having, initially, been sceptical of cameramen's attachment to the 'texture' of film) I now, and without much hope of seeing it restored to documentary budgets, happen to think they're right. Digital video is not the same. Film-effecting is not the same. The plasticity of film (to import a term from art criticism) does better approximate the cognitive wiring we use when we summon up memories, both public and private; often a state of half-dreaming, half-reminiscence, not in any event, in neither case, in sharp, brilliantly crystalline focus. For that very reason, video dogmatists (in the Danish sense) routinely object to what they claim is the dishonestly manipulative quality of film. But, as far as I'm concerned, the moment a shot is framed, something other than the passive recording of 'reality' is being achieved. The *faux*-literalism of the video dogmatists is, in fact, reminiscent of the delusions of historians who persist in believing that somehow the archives write themselves and all they do is point their brains at the sources, exit and write the history. They, too, 'frame' when they pre-formulate the questions they ask of their sources, and their framing is just as much the product of prior preoccupations and prejudices as the video director's.

Taped reconstructions, imprisoned in documentary budgets, make the line between plausibility and giggles perilously fine. This was something the pioneers of television history were obviously acutely aware of. Even with this cautionary lesson, working on periods such as the Middle Ages, where there is little or no rostrum, and even less in the way of portraits that put faces to the names, it is virtually impossible, however, to do without them. How many wide shots full of pregnant emptiness can one shoot? And for all the professionals' distaste of so-called 'trumpet and drum' history, there are huge turning points in history – Hastings, Bannockburn, Edgehill – which can't and ought not, be avoided. So a repertoire of devices (hand-held shots, Super Eight close-ups) are mobilised to convey something of the physical reality of a battle without the need for hundreds of extras at several hundred pounds a head, per day.

Four years ago, when we did it ourselves, no one had yet been brave enough, or foolhardy enough, to try it. And the results in some of our medieval programmes undoubtedly did capture, and keep, a very large television audience. But we're all conscious now, I think, that those techniques have, with repetition, become a cliché and have lost the power to persuade. What might take their place without breaking the bank is a moot point. Computer-generated images might help but as of now, they are almost as much of a strain on budgets as all-out drama or feature film reconstructions.

\*   \*   \*

And yet we do have some models showing us how to convey some of the epic reality of war with relatively modest means. Here are my two favourite examples (one admittedly a movie): Yves Angelo's masterpiece *Le Colonel Chabert* still, after *Chimes at Midnight* (where Orson Welles has no money at all), the most perfect recreation of a historical moment since the war; and the beginning of Kevin Brownlow's 1975 documentary-drama, *Winstanley*, about the Civil War utopian commune of The Diggers. The point I want to make, both to historians and pro-ducers, is that it seems to me that the brilliance of both sequences at capturing the poetics of the past depends on a conceptual, as much as a technical, break-through. Both directors start with an idea that belongs to the essence of the moment – the godly shout of the parlia-mentary armies; their austere thorny way to battle, in the case of Angelo's Napoleonic soldiers; charismatic glamour. They then proceed to undo those ideas in the action – the godly shout turns into ferocity; and you'll see what happens to the glamour. Importantly, they've both had some help storyboarding their idea: Brownlow from Eisenstein's *Alexander Nevsky*, explicitly acknowledged in the music; and for Angelo, Baron Gros's painting of the aftermath of the battle of Eylau in the winter of 1807. Not to mention from Beethoven. Angelo's idea is to show not the battle itself but its immediate aftermath, a moment both of incontrovertible historical truth and poetic pathos.

Between the re-awakened dead and the living steps, the presenter, chorus-like (Derek Jacobi did a dazzling job of this in Kenneth Branagh's *Henry V*) tries somehow to help along the illusion of being lost in the past without being egregiously and annoyingly present. But he can get help in this exercise of creating virtual realities from locations that ought never be merely picturesque or generically suggestive, but which ought to speak simultaneously to story and argument. In the films the place becomes the chorus – not just scene-setter but commentator as well.

In 'Dynasty' (Episode 3) which focuses on Thomas Becket and Henry II, Becket, on the run from the royal wrath, finds refuge in the Cistercian Abbey of Pontigny, south-east of Paris. What we were aiming for here is a glimpse inside Becket's austere, uncompromising mind and as it happens – not coincidentally – Cistercian architecture is the most aus-tere and pure of all the orders, which is why it was largely left alone in the French Revolution. So Clare Beavan, the director, framed the shots with occasional glimpses of me, as if we were indeed not just in a refuge but inside, as it were, not John Malkovich, but Thomas Becket. 'In Victoria and her Sisters' (Episode 13) – in a peculiar way almost like an ecclesiastical aisle – the strategy is deliberately, almost aggressively, counter-suggestible; where the frank visual admission of the ruin of the location – a derelict cotton mill in Ancoats, Manchester – repairs itself in the viewer's imagination. The wreckage has been made by time, but it plays perfectly to the sense of a wrecking crew by human hand that we wanted to imply at this point in the story.

For 'The Two Winstons' (Episode 15) Clare Beavan and I chose our locations with an eye to the poetry of ruins – the boarded-up country house; the extraordinary junkyard housed in one of the big ship repair sheds at Chatham Royal Naval Dockyard; the abandoned Second World War airstrip; even the backlit Wigan coalmine. This was not for cheap pathos. The emptiness of those locations we wanted filled by the viewer's imagination – especially the airstrip and control tower for the 1939–40 sequences, which we very deliberately did not intercut with shots or even sounds of Spitfires and Lancasters. Again, the idea was to make these locations speak to the heart and soul of our film, which was the issue of historicism itself – the virtues and the vices, the riches and the cost of the hardcore British addiction to the past. With the right director and cameraman (and I've been incredibly fortunate to have had both, right through this series) place can be made to speak, to be its own presenter; or even a kind of re-enactor. So can other players who don't need to learn their lines.

Our use of animals isn't an attempt to marry nature films with history – *Walking with Heraldic Beasts*. The proxy effect of using animals and birds emblematically has its roots in the historical sources and its rationale in the stage of both story and argument. In the case of turning Henry II into a bird of prey, we were, of course, alluding to the king's own famous passion for falconry, his notorious predator's instinct; but also to the medieval tradition of bestiary literature in which the persona of kings and bishops, heroes and villains was clad, symbolically, in feathers and fur. The white peacock mixed into the portrait of Elizabeth was to make a point, as economically as possible, about the relationship between display and charismatic authority. And William Cobbett – even physiognomy aside – was often compared to a pig, pungent and mucky, sometimes by himself, and always affectionately. Though we did not use the quote in the film, Cobbett himself wrote that when he was preparing a pigsty for the winter he would occupy it himself for a bit and if he liked it, then he could be sure that the pigs would too.

\*   \*   \*

So these visual strategies are never meant as mere décor. They are all intended to introduce debate by stealth, in ways which flow naturally from both the storyline and the visual storyboard. Sometimes, we introduced visual epigrams at the beginning of our films to which we'd return at the end, creating the on-screen equivalent of a complete narrative arc – the sawn-away ring on Elizabeth's finger inaugurating the debate about the bodies, political and personal (or as contemporaries said 'natural') of the two queens, and ending with the return of that ring to Mary's estranged son James VI, in Scotland.

Without promising too much – or risking hubris – it seems to me, four years after we began, and ten years after I started making documentaries about art and history for the BBC, that television history, done well through the union of provoking commentary and spectacular visual imagination, has nothing to apologise for. If it has the courage of its own convictions, and reinvents its own way of visiting the past, not just struggling to translate the issues of printed history; if it refuses to rest on its laurels but looks for new kinds of stories to communicate; if it re-examines the best ways to engage the imagination whilst stimulating debate; if it does not shrink from contemporary problems, whilst not distorting history to promote them, then it has a fighting chance of realising Macaulay's dream of making a history which is not only 'received by the reason but burned into the imagination'.

# 3
# All Our Yesterdays

*Jeremy Isaacs*

At the front of his novel *An Instance of the Fingerpost*, Iain Pears puts an epigraph from Cicero's *De Oratore*. It reads: '*Historia vero, testis temporum; lux veritatis; vita memoriae; magistra vitae.*' History is a witness to the times we live in; it shines the light of truth; it lends life to human memory; it takes over our lives. These are not bad yardsticks by which to measure history on television.

\* \* \*

I started work for Granada Television, forty-five years ago, in May 1958. I applied to Granada because its owner, Sidney Bernstein, saw broadcasting as part of the democratic process, and insisted that television cameras could and should bear witness to current events, elections for example. At this time the BBC, in the words of its Handbook for 1956, was, between the Dissolution of Parliament and Polling Day, 'careful to exclude from its programmes anything which could fairly be considered likely to influence electors in recording their votes'.[1] Granada proposed, in precisely that period, to bring candidates before the electorate. In February 1958, covering a by-election at Rochdale, Granada persuaded the three political parties to allow their candidates to present their case directly to the electors, by debating with each other, and by answering questions live on television. 'Yours is the sort of television company I'd like to join', I told someone interviewing me for the job. 'I'm not interested in westerns and quizzes.' 'We show the best westerns and make the best quiz-shows on the network', she shot back. But my luck held, and I got the start. The need to balance the ambitious and popular in programming still tests the broadcaster today.

At that time, Granada was experimenting with a documentary technique called action-stills. Still photographs of quality were printed up large, and arranged in sequence. Over them, a rostrum camera hovered, moving in and pulling out, panning and tracking, bringing out significant detail. The camera's movement was intended to convey the illusion of a living reality. The example followed was a documentary on the Klondyke Goldrush by Pierre Berton. In my mind's eye, I can still see a line of black figurines of the hopeful, picked out against the snow, as they climbed high and diagonally left, in search of fortune. Granada was using a fine collection of stills, with music and commentary added, to make a film of *The Boer War*. The camera's movements over the stills was made to appear so natural that when the film-maker, Claude Whatham, introduced the one brief snippet of actual newsreel he had, one hardly noticed the transition, though the newsreel was jerkier. In 1960, in New York with Sidney Bernstein, I met American programme-makers. At NBC, Donald B. Hyatt had made a film using stills of the American Civil War. *Meet Mr Lincoln* lasted half an hour. A gem. In the 1980s, for PBS, Ken Burns' *Civil War* married still images and personal testimonies in letters and diaries. It ran to seventeen hours. A masterpiece.

Back in Manchester, I was given charge, in addition to *What the Papers Say*, of a simple weekly programme *All Our Yesterdays*, based on a deal Granada had done with British Movietone News. We took their newsreels, issued twice a week precisely twenty-five years before, and used them, and no other, in our weekly show. *All Our Yesterdays* was an inexpensive programme; it was intended to entertain, as well as to inform. The first presenter had been James Cameron, whose elegant manner was thought, by Cecil Bernstein, a touch too austere. After a year he gave way to Brian Inglis. I arrived also. Inglis, journalist and historian, was the most unassuming of men. He had a keen mind, and a shrewd judgement. The presenter of *All Our Yesterdays*, catchy theme tune by Ambrose, had little to do but string together whatever Movietone came up with, correct the over-optimistic tone of the newsreel commentator, and set some stories in more realistic context. If an item was merely light relief, we let it play. When desperate for material, we would pad the programme out with a period movie clip; favourite standbys were dance routines by Ginger Rogers and Fred Astaire. But *All Our Yesterdays* could be hijacked on occasion by more serious historical intent. My year in charge, 1961, delivered a prize; it saw the 25th anniversary of the Abdication. Bulking out our source material a little, we devoted the entire programme in successive weeks to this one subject. Inglis went on to write rather a good book on it.

Granada gave me the chance to try my hand at two single, historical documentaries. The first was *The General Strike*; in this, a director Peter Bradford, and the political commentator Henry Fairlie, were my collaborators, though I was a little disconcerted to discover that Fairlie had cribbed a sizeable chunk of his treatment from Charles Loch Mowat's *Britain Between the Wars*. Richard Arnell wrote a lively musical score. There were no interviews, only newsreel and still photographs. We eschewed reconstruction, but filmed footsteps on a Whitehall pavement to cover a diary entry; a hand, toying with a pipe on a desk, signified Baldwin. I found the shot we used for the title sequence, a soldier with fixed bayonet on guard in front of barbed wire in a London street, in the Pathé library, high up under a rooftop in Soho. It was filed under 'Strikes, General'. But was it really London, or Dublin during The Troubles? Afterwards I could never decide, so I had it blown up and hung on my wall to remind me to be careful thereafter. I aimed in *The General Strike* to be even-handed between strikers and establishment. Clancy Sigal dismissed the result, in the *New Statesman*, as pallid and bloodless, a view shared, I discovered, by at least one Bernstein, Sidney's sister. But making the film taught me something of the BBC's role in the event: succeeding in not being taken over by Winston Churchill, but agreeing to keep the Archbishop of Canterbury, thought by government too sympathetic to the strikers, off the air. At the strike's end, and the film's, I used the voice of John Reith, announcing Parry's *Jerusalem*.

The next film I made, *The Troubles*, fostered a lifelong interest in Irish history. My collaborator in this was Brian Inglis, himself a West Briton. Here the footage was more dramatic, the struggle fiercer. But, again, I aimed at a calm rather than committed view of the conflict. When Inglis reported for Granada John F. Kennedy's visit to Ireland, Ulster Television took his commentary off the air, I suppose because they thought it too Irish. But that formidable Ulster Protestant, John Cole, liked *The Troubles*, and wrote to say so.

In both these apprentice projects, I was determined to stay 'in period'. I used no narrator to camera, and no eyewitness accounts. The alternative method of constructing a narrative I ruled out *a priori*, as 'not in period'. This self-denying ordinance could have been limiting, but since there was more than enough material to fill the time slot, I got by. In fact, in both these films I was, without realising it, steering a middle course between two then extant models; images without a historian; the historian solo, without the image's aid. The Pathé library put its archive to use by making newsreel compilations of a year's events, quick-cut round-ups of the striking and the bizarre, entertaining enough, but totally mindless. The films were illustrative of the craft of film editing; history scarcely entered into it. At the other extreme, the first British historian to seek the media limelight, A.J.P. Taylor, stood alone in the studio and talked to camera. Without a prop or a note, without a hesitation or a syllable out of place, Taylor gave a dazzling demonstration of his lecture technique, ending always pat with the point he wished to make, at precisely the right second on the clock; no distractions; just the historian, epigrammatic, provoking, compelling. I take the Pathé series and Taylor's as contrasting parameters. Yet an intelligent talking-head is always *visually* compelling. Taylor's certainly was.

This dichotomy demonstrates that you can have history on television without visual aids, but you cannot have it without a historian's insight. There has to be a mind involved; but the mind need not always be visible. Absence of body does not rule out presence of mind. These days, the historian as television presenter is very evidently with us; Simon Schama, David Starkey and others, command our screens. Watching them, listening to them, we respond to their narrative. Historians may clamour to address the camera; it sells books after all. But the historian involved in television need not always do so, though if he's dealing with the remoter past, pre-photography, it leaves a glaring hole if he doesn't. There are television series in which the historical intelligence operates under cover to determine content or guide interpretation. This mind may be that of a single individual, though that is rare. More likely, watching the credits carefully, you will detect the outline of a college, embracing both advisers and executives, and including researchers, writers and producers. In most – *The Great War, The World at War, Cold War* – there will be both professional historians and an editor with the final say. What there will not be is a void. In any decent television history, single-shot or series, there is a mind in the machine.

\* \* \*

In 1964, like a comet, BBC2's *The Great War* burst into our ken. The scale was prepossessing; there were twenty-six forty-minute episodes. Sir Michael Redgrave narrated. At the heart of its making was a creative tension between the skilled programme-makers, Tony Essex and Gordon Watkins, and the historians employed to shape the argument, John Terraine and Corelli Barnett. This tension, this part-separation of roles and convergence of impact, is well brought out in Professor John

Ramsden's paper to the conference on the series at Queen Mary College, University of London, in 2000, a conference which helped give *The Great War* a new lease of life.[2] Tony Jay of the BBC's Tonight unit, which gave birth to it, saw *The Great War* as potentially a necessary, humane corrective to the insouciant gung-ho of US series like *Victory at Sea*, or Jack Ie Vien's *Churchill: the Valiant Years*. But Ramsden notes that: 'The very choice of lead writers, Terraine and Barnett, already known to take a rather robust attitude to the War, and to the defence of British gener-alship, was indication enough that producers did not actually intend their series to take a pacifist or anti-war line.' Barnett and Terraine, note, were *writers* as well as advisers. However, Ramsden goes on: 'The scripts were well researched and tough-minded but were then yoked to pictures selected for their ability to involve and to move the viewer. A basic ten-sion remained in the series throughout, between a core idea of the war that reflected the best contemporary military history, and a visual and aural presentation' – interviews with veterans, commentary and literary sources – 'that produced from the public an emotional revulsion against all wars, and this one in particular'.

There were additional tensions present. Basil Liddell Hart, the series' military adviser, disagreed strongly with the line taken in programmes on the Somme and Paschendaele, and very publicly resigned. Noble Frankland, Director of the Imperial War Museum, was also displeased. The IWM contracted to supply war footage to the series, and it was pro-vided in the contract that, not trusting the producers an inch, they would have an opportunity to vet each episode, and comment, before it was finalised. Frankland was furious to find, he tells us in *History at War*,[3] that he and his colleagues never saw the programmes until it was far too close to transmission to make effective criticism, or have any input into the broadcast version. He was even angrier at what he thought was irre-sponsible and improper use of reconstructed material, without any visi-ble acknowledgement identifying it as such. He protested to the BBC's Director General, Hugh Greene, too late for the first broadcasts, but forced a disclaimer at the start of each episode when the series was repeated on BBC1. His concerns are set out in his recent *History at War*. When I mentioned them to Corelli Barnett at the Queen Mary conference, he dismissed them as of minor consequence. Tony Essex, however, did make carefree use of film footage, reversed, and repeated in places, over and over, to serve in portraying different battles in different years. All the same, Barnett is right: the argument over archive footage is a minor flaw on a major work. It is a huge boon to have it available at last on VHS and DVD, and now re-broadcast. Ramsden's paper calls attention precisely to the historians' unseen role in *The Great War*'s making. Invisible maybe, negligible by no means. *The Great War*, inbuilt tension and all, remains a striking model of collaboration between television producer and historian.

* * *

When the BBC got round, five or six years later, to the notion of making the obvious sequel, a television history of the Second World War, they inquired if I would be interested in producing it for them. I was indeed, and flattered to be asked. Then I discovered they'd made the same approach to half a dozen others. In any case the funds were not yet set aside. A delay ensued. I was at Thames Television at the time and thought, why don't we do it here at Thames? We did do just that. Two television series, a suggestion from one programme-maker, and a political decision in Whitehall, conspired to make it possible.

The first series that whetted commercial television's appetite for history was *Mountbatten: the Life and Times of Earl Mountbatten of Burma*. This splendid if vainglorious epic – thirteen hours of four cheers for me – was produced by Mountbatten's son-in-law John Brabourne, directed by Peter Morley and written by John Terraine. The IWM was much involved, this time happily so. The series, which was much enjoyed, pioneered a new method of television autobiography; a triple whammy of encomiastic self-praise: carefully selected interviewees would say how well Louis Mountbatten had conducted himself in some vast new responsibility he had undertaken; the commentary would reaffirm that this was indeed the case; the subject himself, modestly accepting the verdict of his peers, would then tell us, in his own words, just how he had done it, and what a success it had all, effortlessly, been. I must remind myself sometime precisely what the *Mountbatten* series had to say about Dieppe, or the Partition of India. I do remember, after it, asking Lord Mountbatten if he had ever in his life made a single mistake. 'No', he said. (*Mountbatten* may have been the model John Birt had in mind when, on his retirement, he proposed a four-part series on his life to BBC2.) It matters, though, as Arthur Marwick has noted, that Mountbatten's view of the great events of his time in which he participated should be placed so handsomely on the record. The point here is that *Mountbatten*'s success helped persuade ITV, and Thames who sold it to the network, that documentary history, on such a scale, could feature in its schedule, without significant loss of audience or revenue.

Another, under-rated but in this context, crucially important, series was Thames's own *The Day Before Yesterday*, a six-part political history of

Britain from 1945 to 1959, produced by Phillip Whitehead, written and narrated by Robert Kee. The historians who acted as advisers were, for the Tory view, John Barnes, biographer of Baldwin, and for Labour, Bernard Donoghue, biographer of Herbert Morrison. Barnes and Donoghue made valuable inputs, in selecting key moments, pointing to eyewitnesses and in underpinning overall balance in the political mine-field. Kee's delivery of his own voice-over narration was urgent, his voice distinctive, his touch cool. To me, more vividly, because more recent than *The Great War*, *The Day Before Yesterday* brought home the exciting possibilities of juxtaposing a precise event on newsfilm, and the participant in it. It helped too that the interviewees were younger, and the newsreel fresher than that of the First World War. Film prompted testimony; eyewitness cued film. The cut from one to the other worked like a succession of minor electric shocks, investing the narrative surface with jolts of energy. This sort of history worked well as television. I knew we should do more of it.

Peter Batty, a documentary maker, wrote to Thames suggesting a military history of the Second World War. As Controller Features, it was my shout. I did not want to commit to, or work to, Batty's treatment. It was too narrowly, too single-mindedly a military history. I wanted instead to display, over what would certainly have to be twenty-six episodes, social and political content that would reflect the total experience of the combatant nations. There would be prologue and epilogue, and exploration of non-narrative, non-military themes: the experience of occupation, the experience of Auschwitz. The Second World War was total war, if not in the UK, then certainly in occupied Europe, in the Soviet Union, in Japan. Civilians suffered more losses than did fighting men and women. So I put Batty's proposal aside.

In mid-February 1971, the Minister for Posts and Telecommunications (middle-distance runner Christopher Chataway) stood up in the House of Commons and announced, after years of pressure for change, and Treasury resistance to it, that the special tax levied on ITV companies would be reduced, and that there would be a review to consider whether its basis should be altered from a levy on revenue – the companies taxed at source – to a tax on profit, the surplus left after expenditures. There was a condition attached: the money thus made available should be spent, and be seen to be spent, on programmes. I went at once to my boss at Thames, Brian Tesler, and he to his, Howard Thomas, and suggested a history of the Second World War. We needed to take the decision and announce it immediately, in case the somnolent BBC should scent danger, recover itself, and get in first. They instantly agreed.

I asked Noble Frankland for the IWM's collaboration, and for his own services as adviser. He readily assented. On the afternoon of 31 March I advised Peter Morley and John Terraine at the BBC – they were now committed to work on their version of such a history there – that we at Thames were going ahead. The next day, 1 April, we started work.

Noble Frankland was to be our sole adviser. I did not want to pay heed to conflicting advice, and saw no need for it in any case. And the IWM would be a principal archive source – though the considerable advantage of that was partially vitiated by the UK's agreement that royalties for the use of war footage, captured by us and held in London, should nevertheless be paid in Germany to Transit Films, at least as far as world rights were concerned. My account of early consultations goes something like this: 'I asked our historical adviser, Noble Frankland, to let me have, on one sheet of paper, or the back of an envelope, fifteen military subjects, the decisive campaigns, which I would not be forgiven if I left out. Each film would treat only one subject – cardinal rule. I had other plans', as I've mentioned, 'for the other eleven programmes. This he did.' I stand by that story, though I doubt I still have the envelope.

Here is Frankland's version set out in his volume *History at War*, (a must-read incidentally for his story of the tenacious assault the Air Ministry and RAF launched on his and Philip Webster's official history of the Strategic Air Offensive to prevent its publication, and of his successful resistance):

> Even before we had reached the necessary formal agreements, Isaacs and I had begun to map out the structure of the series. My first contribution was to observe that the original outline was far too much Europe-orientated and far too little directed towards the problems of the war in the Far East .... I urged too that we should break away from received British prejudices about the war and that, for example, the series should make it clear that the civilians who suffered most were not Londoners nor the people of Coventry, but the Germans from bombing, the Russians from siege and occupation, and the Japanese from both conventional and atomic bombing.
>
> I also wanted it to be made clear that the land operations which decisively exhausted the German army were not in Africa, Italy or France, but in Russia. As to details, even at the outset, I applied the heavy hand to loose drafting. For example, the Germans did not break through the Maginot Line; they circumvented it. Italian naval strength was not destroyed at Taranto; it was reduced, and so on.

Frankland also refers to the overriding architectural problem confronting the producer of a series on a conflict lasting several years – *The World at War*, or indeed an ideological–economic–political conflict lasting decades – *Cold War*. The problem is how to combine, in one continuous narrative, battles that are fought and won in a comparatively brief time-span – events like El Alamein say, or D-Day – with campaigns that last for years – protracted bombing offensives, or the enduring struggle to keep Atlantic sea-lanes open. Or how, in a series on total war, to combine the narrative treatment of successive military campaigns, arranged in chronological sequence, with the thematic treatment of persistent issues or lasting experiences – for example, the strategic conduct of the war, the effectiveness of a combatant nation's war economy, the moral choices open to the individual living under harsh occupation – resist or collaborate – when those experiences and themes have relevance over the entire time-span covered. How do you complete any one of them, without anticipating the final conclusion of the whole? If you opt for twenty-six event-based episodes, the viewer will never see the wood for the trees. If you choose twenty-six themes, each over-arching, you will end with stasis, no sense of forward movement in time, no beginning, middle, progress to an end. No eager anticipation of next week's episode. No narrative. In *The World at War* and *Cold War*, getting that arrangement right was a task I set myself.

Noble Frankland and I agreed well enough. He had plenty of time to read outlines, view rough-cuts and remonstrate with me if he had critical points to make. Individual writers and producers tackled, always within limited air time, historical issues an episode might throw up. Here's David Elstein on 'The Battle for Britain':

> Television history is essentially narrative: it has to tell a story which is clear and to the point. Most historians, on the other hand, present the evidence they have accumulated, weigh it, and reach conclusions based on it. Television history is simply unable to handle material in that way, because the audience cannot be expected to keep several conflicting pieces of evidence in mind while waiting for the programme to reach its conclusion.
>
> A typical example of 'filleting' concerns the Luftwaffe's decision to bomb London on September 7, 1940, instead of the RAF fighter bases. Some historians have suggested that the main reason for this change in tactics was that Berlin had been bombed in August, much to Hitler's anger. The scriptwriter, Laurence Thompson, and I agreed that a more likely reason was that the Luftwaffe assumed the fighter bases

had been put out of action and that, in bombing London, they would either have a clear run, or would force the remaining fighters to defend the capital, and so expose themselves to German gunpower.

In the end, we neither mentioned the retaliation idea, nor why we had excluded it: which was poor history in one sense, but 'good' television in another.[4]

Elstein wrote that in 1974 when television had no recourse except straight linear narrative. Today it is possible, on a set of DVDs, or making use of a dedicated website, to direct the viewer as student immediately to consider other explanations, alternative narratives. CNN's *Cold War* improved on previous best practice by making available on its website an inventory of sources for every image, and the full unedited text of all 550 interviews garnered for the series. But still few programmes formally put forward more than one view. (I know of only one series which practised history as dialectic. *The Dragon has Two Heads*, for Channel 4, saw the marvellous Welsh Marxist, Gwyn Alf Williams, in itinerant debate with traditionalist and romantic Wynford Vaughan Thomas. This short series sparked further argument, and should be imitated.)

Judgement is not the whole of the historian's task. There is also inquiry: to interpret evidence, you must first obtain it. The historian as presenter is his own expert guide to source material. But a history of the twentieth century, say, using eyewitness and newsreel, and doing without a presenter to camera, must find verifiably sourced film, and credible men and women as witnesses. These inquiries are made by the researcher, the key figure on whom the honesty and authority of the completed programmes chiefly depends. On *The World at War* and on *Cold War* I have been fortunate to work with superb researchers. Their contribution is unremarked by the outside world, and undervalued in the industry. Yet it is crucial.

The *World at War*'s film researchers were John Rowe and Raye Farr. Raye Farr describes the task they were set:

1. to illustrate the major events and issues of the war selected for treatment by the producers and historian/writers. In some cases, this meant using the same old film as always because there was no alternative, or because we couldn't get our hands on it due to pressures of time or difficulties of access ...
2. to be as true to the events as possible in our use of the film, so that it did not distort or purposely mislead ...

3. to locate material which matched the recollections and revelations of the contemporary interviews – sometimes confirming, sometimes contradicting, their 'eyewitness' accounts.
4. to provide our editors whenever possible with uncut film so that they might have some freedom to create effective visual sequences, without being hamstrung by the clipped newsreel style of the past, and the heavy hand of the wartime censors.
5. to add to the historical documentation of the period by providing fresh material and new perspectives –
   (a) by going back to the rushes shot by film units of the armed forces and newsreel companies, the offcuts from documentaries, the unused and censored items from all sources
   (b) by sifting through amateur films made available to us
   (c) by searching out all the colour film of the period. There turned out to be far more than we imagined ...[5]

The work was long and onerous. Farr again:

> I suspect that you have never done a really thorough job of film researching in an archive if, when you depart, there is not an audible sigh of relief, fond as it may be, from the staff. Not until you have made a nuisance of yourself do they throw up their hands in exasperation and say, 'See for yourself' – which is what you've been waiting for. (Eventually they're inclined to say, 'Get it yourself ... load it yourself ... rewind it yourself ...') Or better yet, they realise you're still not going and say, 'You've already seen every foot of film we know of on the war, you may as well look at this – we don't know what's in these cans because we've never had time to go through them.' And they reveal a vault of unopened treasures. We are greatly indebted to Herr Homan at the Bundesarchiv in Koblenz for just such an offering.

What Raye Farr showed me, when I joined her at the Bundesarchiv, was material shot behind the German lines on the Eastern front, by a gifted documentary cameraman. He appears not to have been shooting for the newsreel, but out of an urge to document what he saw. Some of his footage was almost idyllic, showing soldiers at rest and leisure. Other sequences were more menacing. He filmed three German soldiers, gently, almost reluctantly, but in the end, firmly clearing a village of its people, sending the men in one direction, the women and children in another. Somehow, you know they will never see each other again.

Here's another aware and enlightening researcher's tip from Farr:

> Instructional films are likely to be very long, and to appear tedious and unpromising. But they can be some of the most rewarding sources, because they deal with the real and immediate problems faced in wartime by fighting men and civilian authorities. They are made for people who know far more than the general public are allowed to know about what is *really* going on. Soldiers know that men die, sometimes hideously, on the battlefield. Films made for the instruction of the army medical corps will contain more realistic elements than newsreels which aim to encourage civilian commitment to a government's war aims.

It was a prime aim of *The World at War* to draw on experience in Hamburg and Berlin, as well as London and Coventry. We needed researchers who spoke German. Susan McConachy, blonde and blue-eyed, was our star. Her hardest task was to track down the SS, and persuade them to talk, on the record. She found Karl Wolff, Himmler's adjutant. Her worst moment was when he put his hand on her knee and confided: 'My dear, you are just the type from whom we liked to breed.' Here is how she treated him:

> My first clue was from a personal contact made by a colleague outside Germany. I had an address near Munich ... Many phone calls, a letter through a third party, and nearly a year later, I finally met the old man. Not in his home, I still didn't know where it was, but in a hotel in Berlin. He was most charming – quite unlike the fantastic figure we had imagined in Munich. Again the long process of establishing trust began. I visited his home several times. He agreed to talk about the subjects where he claimed he had firsthand knowledge. He wanted to explain the ideology of the SS to us. A contract was drawn up which gave him the option to read a transcript of the entire interview to check the factual accuracy of what he had said. The interview was long and tricky. It went on all day. After lunch I asked him to repeat the story he had told me one evening over supper about an incident at Minsk at which he had been present, when 100 people were shot into an open grave as a demonstration for Himmler. He looked a bit surprised. He had forgotten that he had ever mentioned that. Then the film ran out. I wondered if, with time to think, he would actually tell the story again. When we were ready to go he did in fact tell it. I was relieved, not just because I'd got the story, but

because he'd had the time to reflect on what the consequences of telling it might be and I could feel less responsible if he did in fact end up in court again when the programme was shown. Twenty rolls and a lifetime later we left to rush to catch the last plane back to London.[6]

Sue McConachy still had nightmares about her work long after it was finished. The high seriousness of her approach, and the thoroughness of her method, matched, I must say, in every cadre of the production team, were the cornerstones of our success.

*The World at War* took fifty of us three years to make, and is still seen today. It is by no means perfect, or complete. It is well known that there is no explicit mention in it of Enigma or Ultra, only references to an ability 'to crack enemy codes'. We finished work in May 1974. The papers revealing just what happened at Bletchley Park were published two months later, in July. Neal Ascherson, the series' most distinguished writer, has pointed to our neglect of Poland in 1939. And, although we tried to show the crucial importance of the Eastern Front, and the massive contribution the Soviet Union made to the Nazi's defeat, we didn't do it as effectively as we might have done if the Russians had not for two years refused us their cooperation. Richard Overy, in a new introduction to Mark Arnold-Foster's book which accompanied the series,[7] albeit at some remove, reckons that today we would take a harsher view of the Wehrmacht's general behaviour, particularly on the Eastern Front. And he told another Queen Mary College conference – on *The World at War* – that it was now time to take account of new information on low morale and desertion among Allied troops in various theatres. Tellingly, he pointed to the long-lasting and bloody Sino-Japanese war as the single most neglected aspect of a global conflict. But Overy also believes that the scope of *The World at War*'s ambition gave writing historians who might otherwise have preferred to cherry-pick, the courage to embrace in their work the whole panoramic sweep. That had never occurred to me.

Noble Frankland has one regret: he could not persuade me not to use Sir Laurence Olivier to narrate. Actually at first I had not wanted Olivier either, thinking I would use writers with an interest in the war, such as Ludovic Kennedy and Robert Kee, who could also narrate. But Thames, wisely, insisted; for sheer showbusiness oomph, for prestige, and for sales worldwide, we must use Olivier. I readily gave in. After a nightmarish start, he did it marvellously. It is scarcely possible now, given that disparate episodes were creating a unified whole, to re-imagine it without him.

\* \* \*

I did, though, get my chance to work with Robert Kee. After I left Thames, in 1978, the BBC invited me, I guess at Kee's suggestion, to produce a television history of Ireland, which he would write and present. Robert Kee, though Alan Taylor told me he would never finish it, is the author of *The Green Flag*, a history of Irish Nationalism. I leaped at the chance. Here is how the series *Ireland: A Television History* begins:

> Some people think it is dangerous to go into Irish history, because by looking into old troubles you may aggravate new ones. But as a historian of Ireland, Dr A.G. Richey, replied over a hundred years ago to people who made this same charge then: a knowledge of the truth is never dangerous, though ignorance may be so; and still more so is that half knowledge of history which enables political intriguers to influence the passions of their dupes, misleading them with garbled accounts of the past. ... Northern Ireland has had its fair share of political intriguers and their dupes, and more than its fair share of garbled accounts of the past. Ungarbling the past is what this [series] is about.[8]

Kee was no ordinary example of historian as television presenter. He was a television presenter who happened also to be a historian. The advantage showed. No writing historian had or has a better notion of how a television film is put together. The writing of a film, he dinned into me when we first worked together, is first and foremost the making of the film. Pre-planned pieces to camera may set the structure of the argument. In commentary voice-over, the actual words come last. The writing is part of the making, not something separate. An abiding memory of Robert in the making of the series is of him, alone, hunched over the steenbeck, evening after evening, running the pictures back and forward, forward and back, while finding and fitting the words that would best bring out the meaning we intended.

The author of *The Green Flag* would have less need of minders than most, and the series could well have been made without them. But this was a BBC/RTE co-production, and it was plain common sense, and good politics, to consult others. Three historians were recruited. A.T.Q. Stewart, author of *The Narrow Ground*, spoke for Loyalist Ulster. From the University of Cork, Professor John Murphy stood guard for Irish Republicanism. In the centre, from the eminence of Trinity College, Dublin, was its Provost, F.S.L. Lyons, author of one of the best of modern Irish histories. They were indeed consulted, and had scholarly points to make. There were no serious disputes that I recall, and indeed an element of trust prevailed. They knew Robert, knew he knew his stuff, and knew where he was coming from. Stewart was zealous in urging points of emphasis on the Ulster Loyalists' behalf. Lyons was magisterially approving. Murphy was warm, but resigned; this was not the series he would have made. But he picked no quarrels. In the end *Ireland: A Television History* was transmitted, complete and uninterfered with on either side of St George's Channel, although an ordinance of Dail Eireann had to be revoked in Dublin, and permission sought in London from the BBC's Director General Ian Trethowan, before we were permitted to include the utterance of Joe Cahill, recently an active member of the IRA.

We found and interviewed men and women who were 'out' in 1916, and had vivid memories of the Rising. We were glad indeed to find that RTE, in 1966, had filmed (and kept) recollections by relatives of 'the men the British shot' who had visited the death cells the nights before their, staggered, executions. Chillingly, we heard from one of the Collins' murder squad, Vincent Finn, of his part in the events of the original Bloody Sunday, in 1921. We were not short of talk in Ireland, in the twentieth century at least.

The appalling difficulty of making *Ireland: A Television History*, and the fascination of it, lay in the first six of its thirteen hours. At their end, we had reached 1900. We had no film, precious few photographs, and no one to interview. We did have landscape – but what landscape! – ruins, monuments, documents, relics of the past. And, inspiringly, we had Robert Kee, hair carefully combed, or, at Lambay Island or Baginbun, blowing in the breeze. He spoke of what he knew with pith and elegance; voice, language, memorable presence. Without this historian presenter, the series could not have been made. But we needed some visual variety, and there were gaps that we necessarily struggled to fill. We set our face against reconstructions. Instead, we sometimes used the present as metaphor for the past. Thus, to represent the battle at the Yellow Ford, we showed a hurling match in full melee. I wince still when I think of it. Nowadays when I notice the persuasive narrative of Simon Schama's *History of Britain*, interrupted, not now and again, but again and again, by the nondescript, whippanned blur of invented battle, I sympathise with him, and with the director and editor involved.

\*   \*   \*

Minding my own business at the Royal Opera House, I received an emissary from Ted Turner, owner of CNN. He wanted a history of the Cold

War, and wanted me to make it. I could not, and said so. But, later, I realised that, with others on board, and particularly if I could prevail on Martin Smith to do the serious work as series producer, I might be of some help in getting it made. When I met Ted Turner in Atlanta, he stressed he didn't want a triumphalist approach, but a narrative that would reflect a generation's experience in the US, and USSR and, I urged, in Europe. We shook hands on that, there and then, though only after I'd insisted that the forty episodes he thought were needed to do the subject justice were twenty or so too many. Martin Smith recruited a highly effective team, and in autumn 1995 production began. *Cold War* went to air on CNN and BBC2 in late 1998, by which time I had been eighteen and more months away from Covent Garden. *Cold War*, for which with Pat Mitchell of Turner Original Productions I served as executive producer, had three principal historical advisers: Laurence Freedman, Head of the Department of War Studies at King's College, London; Vladislav Zubok, a post-Soviet, Russian historian, then at George Washington University, Washington DC; and, then at Athens, Ohio, now at Yale, the distinguished Cold War historian, John Gaddis. We also benefited hugely from the newly published researches of the Cold War International History Project at the Woodrow Wilson Institute, and from the advice and help of Tom Blanton and Bill Burr at the National Security Archive. Freedman, Zubok and Gaddis studied every outline, viewed every fine cut, read every final commentary script, and commented on each in fine detail. Martin Smith responded to each message, reconciling the whole with miraculous tact. There were a few disagreements, patiently resolved. There were no explosions. It was a happy ship.

When *The World at War* was over, one British historian told an IWM conference, bringing together historians and television people, that he'd viewed the tapes and junked them, since there was nothing in them of interest to his students. When Taylor Downing went to ask John Gaddis whether he would advise us on *Cold War*, he said he would; he used *The World at War* as a teaching tool for students. He went on to use *Cold War*, in fine cut, at Yale, and had to move classrooms to accommodate his audiences. In the US, the neo-con right hated *Cold War*, having it in from the start for Ted Turner who went duck-shooting with Fidel Castro, their particular bête noire. *Cold War* was denounced as lies, though no specific falsehood was cited. Coming close to the present, always dangerous for history, we ran into the cross-fire of ideological, political controversy. The neo-cons wanted precisely the triumphalist version of events Ted Turner and I believed could be improved on. They objected to the prominence we attached to Gorbachev's role in ending it. But, in fact, we showed the USA rich, well-armed, self-confident, keeping the pressure of arms expenditure up, and facing down its adversary, a USSR that was poor, backward, inefficient and, as shown in the event, literally falling apart. The brunt of Cold War suffering was in Soviet-dominated Eastern Europe. I gave the last word to Vaclav Havel, who knew the rottenness of the communist system from bitter experience. He lived under it; *testis temporum.*

## Notes

1. BBC Handbook, 1956.
2. 'The Great War: The Making of the Series', J. A. Ramsden. *Historical Journal of Film, Radio and Television*, vol. 22, no. 1, 2002.
3. *History at War*, Noble Frankland, dlm, 1998.
4. '*The World at War*' SFTA (now *BAFTA*) *Journal*, 1974, included with *World at War* DVD, 30th anniversary edition, Fremantle.
5. *SFTA Journal*, 1974.
6. *SFTA Journal*, 1974.
7. *The World at War*, Mark Arnold-Foster, with a new introduction by Richard Overy, Pimlico, 2001.
8. *Ireland: A Television History*, Robert Kee, Weidenfeld & Nicolson, 1980; revised and updated, Abacus History, 1995.

# 4
# Why is So Much Television History about War?

*Roger Smither*

The answer to the question posed by the title is, I wish to suggest, to be found in the interaction of two subsidiary questions.[1] First, why is the subject of military history attractive to those who commission and make factual television programmes? Second, why do the resulting programmes find and satisfy enough of an audience to justify their continuing production? This chapter confines its consideration of the topic to the experience of the United Kingdom, and refers only to television history programmes that have been broadcast on British terrestrial television – although at least two major series of non-British origin are included in this category. Some of its generalisations may well be true for other countries, but this is an area where conclusions are left to the reader.

\* \* \*

Television schedulers and commissioning editors tend, like their more famous opposite numbers the studio bosses and film producers in Hollywood, to be reluctant to experiment or innovate. Putting a different spin on the doctrine that 'Nothing succeeds like success', the most comfortable belief for them to adopt is that very little succeeds except success – in other words, the best guarantee that a project will make you money, or at least will not lose you money, is to ensure that it conforms closely to the pattern of something that has visibly worked before. In the field of British television history, the pattern for success was set in 1964, when the BBC made the twenty-six-part series *The Great War*.[2] This series established both the audience-appeal of warfare as a subject for documentary or historical programme-making and a classic model for delivering that subject-matter. The model has changed little in the ensuing forty years.

The achievement of *The Great War* was the more remarkable in that the series was made by the team behind *Tonight*, a current affairs programme (of which the future BBC Director General Alasdair Milne was then editor), in the days before there was an acknowledged historical documentary strand at the BBC. The project formed part of the launch of BBC2, the Corporation's new 'highbrow' channel. These facts clearly contradict the opening premise of this section – *The Great War* was remarkably innovative and experimental television – but in the context of launching a whole new channel even the more hesitant managers may be bold enough to push the edges of the envelope. Among the lavish production values and features that *The Great War* brought to a new pitch in television history were: extensive research in the film archives of several countries (series documentation records the use of material from more than thirty archives and libraries in over fifteen countries); a large number of excellent interviews with survivors and witnesses of the events portrayed, recorded at a time when the majority of those interviewed were still in their sixties or seventies (the Imperial War Museum Sound Archive has some 275 *The Great War* BBC interviews conducted in 1963–64 listed in its catalogue); the use of the voices of 'star' actors, particularly for the linking narration of each programme, which was spoken by Sir Michael Redgrave, but also to voice the words of key participants, for example, Emlyn Williams as Lloyd George, and Sir Ralph Richardson as Sir Douglas Haig; and thought-provoking scripts, by established or rising luminaries of First World War history and other fields, the major contributions coming from John Terraine and Correlli Barnett but with additional script credits to Alistair Horne, Barrie Pitt and Anthony Jay, among others.

The series also claimed to be treating its archive film with unprecedented respect. Thanks to the technique known as 'stretching' (which some of *The Great War*'s publicity suggested had been discovered and developed specially for the series, although in fact it had been known to the film industry for thirty years or more), it was possible to inter-cut silent archive film, shot at speeds of about sixteen frames per second, with modern sound film shot at twenty-four frames per second, without it having the speeded-up caricature effect with which silent film had tended to be associated since the arrival of sound. The series also laid claim to a very high standard of pictorial authenticity – principally by carrying on-screen a message confessing to occasional minuscule and unavoidable lapses from that standard. A typical example read:

> A very small part of the film material used in this series is reconstructed, usually by Official Photographers two or three days after the

events depicted. Material of this kind is used only where it faithfully reflects the reality and where no genuine film exists.

In point of fact, the series' use of archive film is one of the sticks with which it is easiest to beat it, as the programmes make extensive use of film that falls far short of the self-professed standard of authenticity. Footage is imported wholesale from training films, from later campaigns and other fronts, and from post-war feature films and semi-documentary reconstructions. Given the paucity of authentic combat film from the first fifteen months of the war, particularly from the British Army on the Western Front, and the fact that the series devotes about a third of the total number of programmes to this period, it could hardly be otherwise. The producers also allowed the manipulation of the film to make the programmes more interesting or easier to follow. There was, for example, an effort to ensure that, as far as possible, Allied troops would be seen moving from left to right across the screen while Germans moved from right to left, to match the usual directions of attack on the Western Front as seen on maps. The fact that this required reversing several shots and so produced whole battalions of seemingly left-handed soldiers using rifles which were never made in the configuration shown was considered an acceptable price to pay to avoid confusing the audience.

Retrospective criticism of this type is, however, beside the point compared to the important fact that the series was both a popular and a critical success, and established a model – including allegedly respectful use of archive film – to which future programme-makers could point with confidence when trying to suggest a particular project. They might have been hampered in this by the fact that *The Great War* vanished from the world's television screens shortly after it had been screened. Made in an era when television was still a largely live and repeat-free medium, the producers had no reason to anticipate endless re-runs, let alone domestic sales, and failed to make agreements with those involved which would facilitate such usage. *The Great War* was destined to vanish from the mass audience's reach, if not from its memory, for some thirty-five years. But its tradition was to live on in the success in 1974 of a still more ambitious series on the Second World War – Jeremy Isaacs' production for Thames Television of *The World at War*.[3]

Although Isaacs also cited other precedents, the Thames series consciously replicated the style and the scale of the BBC's, and indeed *The World at War* employed several of those who had worked on the earlier project.[4] The lavish production values were the same, but more so. Sir Laurence Olivier triumphantly assumed the narrator's mantle of

Sir Michael Redgrave. The quantity and quality of the archive research were impressive – the website for the series speaks of researchers going through three million feet of archive film. The website also mentions the accumulation of nearly a million feet of interview and location material – naturally, for events less than thirty years old, the survivors available to the series included a wider range of political and military leaders than had been there for *The Great War*. As 'history' the Thames series worked hard to avoid the mistakes of its predecessor, using film for the most part as conscientiously as it used other documentary sources, and drawing specific attention to questions of accuracy in some of the scenes depicted.

*The World at War* became probably the most successful television history series ever made, broadcast in almost one hundred countries around the globe, frequently many times over, to the extent that it has been in almost constant circulation for thirty years. So great is this success, indeed, that this one series provides part of the answer to the question posed by the title of this chapter – less 'why is so much television history about war?' than 'why is so much television history *The World at War*?' The major contribution of Isaacs and his team to the debate, however, was to confirm the impression created by *The Great War*: that archive- and interview-based television history of warfare could be hugely successful in terms both of audience and prestige. When Ted Turner planned his epic series on *The Cold War* (CNN, 1998),[5] it was specifically *The World at War* that he sought to emulate – bringing in Isaacs, by now Sir Jeremy, to lead the project as executive producer, and involving many other *World at War* alumni. *The Cold War*, however, was simply the largest project to seek to follow the path which the BBC and Thames Television had laid down. The number of other series and programmes made in the same mould is almost impossible to count.

Continuing the tradition of a successful major series recasting (rather than breaking) the mould in which smaller programmes could also shape themselves, the third production to shape the course of television history arrived in 1990. *The Civil War*,[6] directed by Ken Burns, who also co-produced the series for PBS with his brother Ric, built on the successful pattern created by *The Great War* and *The World at War*, but added some important new elements to the mix. Most obviously, as the series dealt with events that were well over a century old, and which preceded by three decades the invention of cinematography, there were no veterans to interview, and no archive films to use. Ken Burns' solution to this in pictorial terms was to make extensive use of atmospheric location shooting and of archival still images, carefully filmed on a rostrum camera. The absence of original sound was made good by using actors reading from contemporary letters and diaries. Actors had been used before, mainly to provide the voices for dead statesmen and commanders, but this approach provided an opportunity to associate still more high-profile acting and other spoken-word 'talent' with the project. Voice credits for *The Civil War* included Laurence Fishburne, Morgan Freeman, Jeremy Irons, Derek Jacobi, Garrison Keillor, Arthur Miller, Pamela Reed, Jason Robards, Studs Terkel, M. Emmet Walsh and Sam Waterston, each of them capable of delivering other people's words better than those people could probably do themselves.

In the wake of *The Civil War*, archive film and 'geriatric talking heads' became optional rather than mandatory features of television history. Film and picture librarians, and commissioning editors, came to lose count of the number of programme-makers who told them that their project 'would do for my topic what Ken Burns had done for the Civil War'. In particular, the Ken Burns approach kept alive the possibility of covering the First World War as the number of actual survivors of that war inevitably declined. The PBS series *The Great War and the Shaping of the Twentieth Century* (re-versioned by the BBC for British transmission as *1914–18*) was the major example in the 1990s.[7]

The years since 'The Civil War' have seen the addition of two further elements to the pattern of accepted success in television history. *The Second World War in Colour*,[8] made in 1999 by Trans-World International for Carlton, with *The World at War* veteran Martin Smith as its Executive Producer, conformed to type in many ways. It had a celebrity narrator, in this case John Thaw, in the style of *The Great War*, and it used readings from letters and diaries, as *The Civil War* had done. Its innovation, however, was to introduce to the airwaves the concept that a programme had added interest if it sought out colour images of events and periods that were more commonly recalled in black and white. Since a large proportion of available colour material was privately shot by amateurs while professionals recorded actuality for the most part in black and white, *The Second World War in Colour* validated 'home movies' as an additional source of history. This series staked a claim to a seam of further topics for similar careful exploration of the world of authentic colour records by the original TWI team, as well as a number of lookalike projects. It also opened the door for a rival series to experiment with the effect of electronically adding colour to originally monochrome film – the 2003 Nugus-Martin Production (for Channel 5) of *World War I in Colour*.[9] It is too early to say whether colorisation, which many welcomed but some saw as violating principles about the ethical use of archive footage, has or will become part of the accepted face of television history.

The other new model established by a history series at the end of the century came with Simon Schama's major BBC project *A History of Britain* (three series, the first broadcast in autumn 2000).[10] These programmes successfully used two techniques that marked important departures from the 'established' methods previously described. By featuring a presenter who spent much of the time on screen himself, the need for other talk-ing heads (whether those of surviving witnesses or other experts) was substantially reduced. At the same time, the use of re-enactment groups to provide atmospheric and reasonably authentic representations of life and combat in particular historic periods broke the chain of reliance on archive film. Schama's series were not breaking new ground in either of these areas – some viewers might recall the engagingly crude historical re-enactments featured in the 1950s series *You Are There* (CBS, 1953–57, introduced by Walter Cronkite), others the impressive achievements on a shoestring budget of Peter Watkins' *Culloden* (made for the BBC in 1964),[11] while Professor Richard Holmes's BBC series of *War Walks* (1996–97)[12] provided just one recent example of several earlier pro-grammes that had placed historians on the ground they were talking about. As with *The Civil War*, however, the effect of *A History of Britain* was to create a new set of norms within which television history could be shown to be both popular and respectable – and as with *The Civil War*, the new norms could stretch back beyond the birth of cinema.

Since *A History of Britain*, another string to the television historians' bow – and one which has the potential to free them from re-enactment societies as well as from archive film – has become apparent in the grow-ing use of computer-generated visuals. Previously most strikingly seen in the BBC's pre-historic natural history series *Walking with Dinasours* (1999) and in feature films, Common Gateway Interface (CGI) was an important ingredient in one evocation of ancient Egypt and two of ancient Rome broadcast by the BBC in the autumn of 2003: *Pyramid*, *Pompei – the Last Day*, and *Colosseum – Rome's Arena of Death*. The last two were reported to have been watched by audiences of over ten and seven million respectively.[13]

The established if slowly changing pattern of acceptable models for television history, built for forty years on the two foundation stones of archive film and oral testimony, subsequently stretched to include other forms of picture and sound, may finally be changing. Historians can think about how good they might look on television, and re-enactment societies wonder whether they should advertise for an agent while CGI experts roll out the welcome mat; critics and commissioning editors can anticipate at last the possibility of television history that pauses somewhere in the long years between 'the dinosaurs and the Nazis'. Meanwhile, film archives and footage libraries must start to wonder whether the regular supply of interest that had come their way since *The Great War* might finally be starting to dry up. However, the possibility of changing patterns in the future leaves unanswered the question of why so much of the past four decades of television history has been devoted to warfare.

It was argued at the start of this chapter that a series or programme is most likely to be made if those putting up the money for it believe that it will emulate the success of something that has gone before. In so far as the major models of success examined above in this period have been series about war – of all those named, only Schama's did not have the word in its title – there is a kind of flying-by-autopilot in this: the successful predecessor was about war, therefore the next series should be as well. However, the series named were not the only programmes to make a major impact in terms of ratings and prestige in this period. Some of the others anticipated by decades the 'innovations' of more recent history, particularly in the field of personality-led series. (Lord) Kenneth Clark's *Civilisation* (1969) and Professor Jacob Bronowski's *Ascent of Man* (1973)[14] were just two major non-military BBC series that matched the success of *The Great War*. The question still remains, therefore: just why was it that war continued to dominate the field of television history?

\* \* \*

It is not only the fact that archive film has been associated with seriously successful previous programmes that makes it attractive to programme-makers. A bigger attraction is that it is generally considerably cheaper to re-use footage that somebody else has already shot than it is to send out a crew to shoot footage from scratch.[15] There are thus commercial as well as critical reasons to make archive-based programmes, which are reinforced by the fact that the majority of film archives are resolutely not-for-profit, if not actually public-sector, organisations. In the USA, with its traditionally generous interpretation of the concept of freedom of information, this places large quantities of archive footage held by two institutions (the Library of Congress and the National Archives) officially in the public domain, with costs limited to the expense of copying. The European tradition is less openhanded, and in Britain at least the arrival of freedom of information legislation postdates several years of government policy that has resolutely encouraged public sector bodies to raise as much as possible of their own funding by revenue-generating activities. Even in Europe, however, enough of a tradition of public service has survived to ensure that full-blown profiteering is held in check. Market pressures between such public sector archives and footage libraries in private hands, as well as competition between the latter, generally helps also to keep prices down and the product affordable. Within this overall picture, there are, nonetheless, some kinds of archive-based programmes that are easier to make than others.

The image of film archives since the supposed birth of the film archive movement in the mid-1930s at the hands of pioneering figures like Iris Barry of The Museum of Modern Art in New York, Ernest Lindgren of the British Film Institute's National Film Library (as it was at the time), and Henri Langlois of the Cinémathèque Française, has most commonly been promoted in terms of a romantic quest to preserve and restore the crumbling heritage of feature films – film as art, or the art of film. In fact, the early theoretical arguments in favour of the preservation of film, and the first practical steps to do something about it, paid scarcely any attention at all to the artistic merits of cinema production, but concentrated instead on the value of film as a historical record. The title of the celebrated pioneering essay *Une nouvelle source de l'histoire* by Boleslaw Matuszewski (published in Paris in 1898) says it all.[16] Fortunately for future television historians, the first actual attempts to create collections of films with an eye to posterity – all of which pre-dated the activities of Barry, Lindgren and Langlois by between fifteen and twenty-five years – were made firmly in the Matuszewski spirit.[17]

What exactly were the films that accumulated in these early libraries and archives of moving pictures? Self-evidently, they were pictures of life after the invention of moving image technology – in other words, pictures of life from the late 1890s onwards. As those decades have seen ten years given over to two cataclysmic world wars, a further forty given over to a Cold War that occasionally turned hot, and an almost continuous succession of smaller wars in the various causes of colonialism, anti-imperialism, *Lebensraum*, self-determination, liberation, revolution, *coup d'état*, counter-insurgency, humanitarian intervention and anti-terrorism, it might well be argued that an emphasis on warfare in archive-based television history is an inevitable reflection of the past century's major preoccupation. There is some truth in this, although it needs to be explained in slightly more complex terms than those of the prevalence of conflict in the twentieth and twenty-first centuries.

Whatever Matuszewski and other theorists might have hoped, the notion of dispassionate filming for the public record has rarely made much impact on the amount of celluloid or videotape that actually passes through cameras. Historically, the major motivations for shooting non-fiction film have been the same as that for shooting fiction or any other kind of film: to entertain. While acknowledging the subsidiary motivations of aesthetic enlightenment, of training and education, and of direct and indirect selling, whether of actual product or of ideas, the major impulse behind all film production has been to satisfy the expectations of paying customers. In non-fiction terms, the principal vehicle for this impulse has been the newsreel, but, in the words of film historian Terry Ramsaye writing in 1934, 'The newsreel is not a purveyor of news and never is likely to become one.... The newsreel ought to be an entertaining and amusing derivative.... Whether they know it or not, the newsreels, as they call them, are just in the show business.'[18]

To paraphrase Ramsaye, the newsreel rarely if ever broke the news: that function was fulfilled by the newspaper or radio, and at best the newsreel provided the moving pictures to fill out a story that was already familiar. The newsreel was also rarely if ever the major motivation for going to a show: more commonly, it was a minor part of an evening's or afternoon's entertainment. The ticket-buying members of the public did not want their mood upset by anything too disturbing, and the manager of the cinema certainly did not want anything controversial enough to provoke bad feelings or a walk-out among his patrons. In both Britain and America, cinema's general avoidance of criticism of the rise of Fascism and Nazism in Europe in the 1930s has become notorious in hindsight.[19] The typical newsreel was almost required to be bland – to concentrate on state occasions, with parades and picturesque ceremonial at home or tours to exotic places overseas, on sport, on technological innovations, on fashion shows and beauty pageants, on celebrities, and on whimsical stories involving children or animals. The only allowable exception to the bland was the spectacular, the latter often meaning disasters, whether natural or man-made. The last group might include a brief visit to a war between two foreign countries, but such coverage tended to be in the spirit of that given to floods, earthquakes and volcanic eruptions – a matter for passing concern or sympathy, but not something to be lingered over. (This familiar profile led Oscar Levant actually to define a newsreel as 'a series of catastrophes, ended by a fashion show'.[20])

When these stories are recycled as archive film a few decades later, it is hard work to find much scope for the production of major series. One-off programmes, featuring celebrity biographies or period vignettes are possible, but extended use is difficult in all categories but one: that of wars involving the home country. A war in which the audience, their families and their country were directly implicated provided the only context which changed the rules for the newsreels. The audience was concerned and involved, and anxious for an insight into the way things were going. Production companies would wish to be seen to be doing their patriotic duty as well as giving the viewers what they wanted. Government would also be concerned to make sure that the audience received that insight in a way that would sustain morale and help the war effort. On the negative side, this might mean censorship and overt propagandising; on the positive side, it tended also to mean an expansion of facilities for shared or pooled newsreel coverage under official control, supplemented by input from official film units.

In the years since the Second World War, with the replacement of newsreels by television news, the picture has changed less than might be anticipated. In the era of '24-hour news', much of what actually appears on the screen is made up of studio analysis and prediction, of repeated highlights of footage that was of interest, and of live feeds and reports from camera crews and journalists waiting for something to happen, generally in stories of local and transitory interest at best. Crises in which the home country is not engaged are visited occasionally, but are not often covered in depth. A 'CNN effect' has been discerned in a few cases, but even when that effect or other causes turn a third-party war into one involving the home country as combatant or peace keeper, media interest does not much outlast the actual fighting. Only a major crisis or a war in which the home country is actively engaged continues to break the pattern. When such a war is in train, its coverage tends to dominate all other news and that coverage is still facilitated and augmented – and controlled – by government and service agencies. Future historians will not find the character of the archived news material, as distinct from the quantity or the technology, all that different from current practitioners.

Feeding through into the archives for future historians to use, this tends to mean that wars generate larger volumes of material than other events, and that a higher proportion of that material is unencumbered by private copyright. To the reasons of economy that make archive film in general attractive to programme-makers, in other words, it is possible to add reasons of interest and quantity to explain why film of war is likely to feature largely in archive-based programming.

\*   \*   \*

Whether programme-makers have been motivated by the vision of what has been successful before, or driven by the economic pressures of what is most easily, cheaply and plentifully available in the archives, they are also constantly at the mercy of the audience: if nobody actually watches a programme, or if the viewing figures are disappointing, it may be withdrawn, and at the very least it will be unlikely to be replicated. Even at the time of *The Great War*, viewers had two other channels to watch if the series did not appeal to them. In 2004 the choice is far greater – and yet in 2004 there are programming strands on 'general' channels as well as dedicated channels which are all given over specifically to catering for an interest in frequently war-based history. At least to some extent, therefore, it must be concluded that the reason so much television history is about war is that this is exactly the way a significant part of the viewing public wants it to be.

Various interpretations of popular culture have been invoked to explain why this might be the case. Where Britain is concerned, that culture is felt to comprise an unhealthy cocktail of xenophobia, especially as directed against continental neighbours, and nostalgia. The latter encompasses both past imperial glories and a range of other features now considered lost to the nation: the innocence of Edwardian England abruptly terminated by *The Great War* (and sometimes more specifically the image of the 'lost generation' of those who died in that war), or the sense of community of sacrifice and commitment evoked by the 'Dunkirk spirit' or the 'blitz spirit' of the Second World War. This chapter is concentrating on the British experience, but other 'national cultures' may respond to war-based television history too. In Australia and New Zealand, the participation of soldiers in the two world wars (and particularly in the ANZAC landings at Gallipoli in the First) is a cornerstone in the building of a sense of national identity. An interesting interpretation of the Second World War has been advanced in America, where a sense of pride in achieving victory over an enemy that undoubtedly needed to be vanquished and was defeated conclusively has been claimed to make the Second World War 'The Good War' in explicit or implicit contrast to the less clear-cut, less conclusive conflicts that have followed it.[21] Similar patterns are discernible in other countries, meaning that an urge to revisit past conflicts can fit comfortably into a wide spectrum of interests and concerns.

Leaving aside the always questionable issue of national character or culture, other characteristics of military history may be invoked to explain its enduring or recurrent popularity. One is the sense of clarity and familiarity that provides the backbone of the subject, in contrast to many or most other historical topics that might be imagined. The audience may on the whole, and not least because of the number of programmes they have already watched on the subject (there is always this element of circularity in all these arguments), be expected to know before the programme begins at the very least who was on which side in whichever war is featured, and what the outcome was. With relatively little need for context, the programme can get down to business more quickly. Against a background of such familiarity, its makers can choose a number of different variations for their approach. They can show an established subject in a new light (for example, by the use of 'in colour' film), or open up a little-known or previously secret aspect of the conflict – the single most conspicuous omission of *The World at War* was caused by the fact that the series was made just before the revelations about the successes of Polish and British code-breakers in cracking the German enigma codes, leaving the way clear for *The Secret War* (BBC 1977)[22] and other such series. Programmes can focus on a detail or paint on the broadest of canvases; they can explore personalities or examine technology. They can conform to preconception or advocate a revisionist view – or in some cases do both at once: *The Great War* was remarkable in its use of images which conformed to preconceptions of mud and futility combined with commentaries which foreshadowed 'revisionist' doctrine on the evolution of tactics during the conflict. The viewers may agree or disagree with the thrust of any one programme but will normally find little difficulty in absorbing it into their general understanding of the subject. In this sense, it will of course become part of the background they bring to the next programme…

But to treat the issue of the popularity of war-based television history solely in terms of popular culture or individual familiarity is to overlook an important third ingredient. It bears repeating that television history based on moving image archive pictures must by definition be recent history; self-evidently, the same must be even more true of television history that aims to include interviews specifically recorded for the programme concerned. Since television history has been largely constructed around these two pillars for the last forty years, it has for the most part been concerned with a period, and with topics, which will resonate in the memories of a large part of the audience, and with the family tradition of most of the rest of it – if the viewer does not personally recall the period, he or she will most probably remember a parent or grandparent who lived through it. In other words, history on the screen reacts with the workings of memory and tradition within the watching audience.

The mechanics of human memory are an area in which I have no expertise whatsoever, but personal observation within my own family, confirmed by anecdotal evidence gleaned from friends and other contacts, leads me to risk the following generalisation. The generations that fought and survived the two world wars grew up in a culture that dealt with involvement in traumatic or even merely unpleasant events by 'moving on' and by expecting survivors – or by survivors themselves expecting – 'not to talk about it'. Many survivors stayed silent for decades after experiencing such horrors as combat on the Western Front in the First World War, or the Holocaust in the Second. At the same time, there seems to be in most of us a powerful urge not to depart this life without telling our story, and people who have 'moved on' for years will quite often wish to 'talk about it' after all as they reach their eighth decade of life. There is, I suggest, a complex interaction that means that the recollection of major world events in television history – and few events were as major as the two world wars – connects with the exploration of personal histories within families and communities. The veteran or survivor talking on the screen encourages the veteran or survivor in the home to tell his or her story – or the sight of the former encourages those surrounding the latter to ask the 'What did you do in the war?' question.

This is a difficult topic, with many chicken-and-egg issues to add to the confusion. To what extent does television history either stimulate or respond to an atmosphere of more general sharing of memories? Is the burgeoning interest in family history in the United Kingdom and elsewhere another contributory factor, or another response? Is the perception of an obligation to testify publicly to particular events – most powerfully in the bearing of witness to the Holocaust – an independent phenomenon or a part of the same continuum? I must repeat that I have no expertise in this area at all, but it seems to me that the concentration of television 'history' on the recent past and the importance of the two world wars in the memory and tradition of people forming the audience for such programmes are inevitably phenomena that operate on each other in some fairly complicated ways.

\* \* \*

In answering the question of why so much television history is about war, one must start with the issues as viewed from the perspective of the makers of such programmes, noting that programmes based on archive footage have been relatively cheap to make, and that warfare offers one of the richest seams to mine in the world's film archives, and going on to observe that such programmes have a long tradition of both critical and popular success behind them. From the producers' point of view, why change a winning formula? This does, however, only answer part of the question: we may know why programmes are made, but why do they continue to be popular? Here we are on more tentative ground. At one level, the subject is easy to grasp, and may, in different ways, be expected to resonate with one aspect or another of the audience's cultural background. There is, however, another level which is more difficult to quantify, which is that such programmes may serve some useful, almost therapeutic, function as a conduit for personal, family and community memories. In this way, perhaps even the most cynical commissioning editor may have been doing some good after all.

## Notes

1. The views expressed in this chapter are personal, and do not in any way represent an official opinion or policy of the Imperial War Museum. I am grateful to Paul Sargent and Jerry Kuehl who took the time to read early drafts of this text, and whose advice, encouragement, corrections and suggestions have been extremely helpful. Their help to me should not, however, be taken as indicating that they necessarily endorse my opinions, or that they should share the blame for any remaining errors: the latter, in particular, is entirely mine.
2. *The Great War* is available for purchase in the UK on VHS and DVD from DD Video. A website devoted to the series is under development but is not yet live. *The Historical Journal of Film, Radio and Television* (Vol. 22, No. 1, March 2002) contained five articles about *The Great War* originating as papers given at a one-day conference on the series at Queen Mary College, University of London on 4 July 2000. John Terraine's illustrated history *The Great War 1914–1918* was published by Hutchinson in 1965; a book by Correlli Barnett, *The Great War* ('based on the classic TV series'), was published by the BBC in 2003.
3. *The World at War* is frequently repeated on a variety of channels, and is available for purchase in the UK on VHS and DVD from Fremantle Home Entertainment. A website devoted to the series under development at http://www.theworldatwar.com/ will provide links to further references. The book of the series, by Mark Arnold-Foster, was published by Collins in 1973.
4. Jerry Kuehl, himself one of those who worked on *The World at War* after *The Great War*, recalls that 'Jeremy [Isaacs] has always explicitly mentioned both the Granada [programmes] *Cities at War* and *All Our Yesterdays* as being very much in his mind when he set out to make [*The World at War*]' (email to Roger Smither, 26 November 2003). *Cities at War*, a three-part series directed by Michael Darlow looking at the Second World War experiences of London, Berlin and Leningrad, was broadcast in November 1968. Introduced by Brian Inglis, the newsreel-based *All Our Yesterdays* ran throughout the 1960s and

early 1970s, and produced at least one spin-off book: Brian Inglis and Bill Grundy, *All Our Yesterdays: How the Newsreels Saw Them from Munich to the Berlin Airlift. From the Granada TV Series,* published by Orbis, 1974.

5. *The Cold War* has been available for purchase in the UK on VHS from DD Video. The CNN website has a special section for the series at http://www.cnn.com/SPECIALS/cold.war/ which provides links to further references. The book of the series, by Jeremy Isaacs and Taylor Downing, was published by Little, Brown in 1998.

6. *The American Civil War,* the British title of *The Civil War,* is available for purchase in the UK on VHS and DVD from DD Video. The PBS website has a special section for the series at http://www.pbs.org/civilwar/ which provides links to further references. The book of the series by Geoffrey C. Ward, with Ric Burns and Ken Burns, was published by Alfred A. Knopf in 1990.

7. *1914–18,* the British version of *The Great War and the Shaping of the 20th Century,* has been available for purchase in the UK on VHS from DD Video: the 're-versioning' carried out by the BBC means that there are significant differences between this and the original US version, which may be acquired from the USA. The PBS website has a special section for the series at http://www.pbs.org/greatwar/ which provides links to further references. The book of the series, by Jay Winter and Blaine Baggett, was published in America by Penguin and in Britain (again with the variant title *1914–18: The Great War and the Shaping of the 20th Century*) by BBC Books in 1996.

8. *The Second World War in Colour* is available for purchase in the UK on VHS and DVD from Carlton Visual Entertainment. The book of the series by Stewart Binns and Adrian Wood was published by Pavilion Books in 1999.

9. *World War I in Colour* is available for purchase in the UK on VHS and DVD from Fremantle Home Entertainment. The book of the series, historical consultant Charles Messenger, was published by Ebury Press in 2003.

10. *A History of Britain* is available for purchase in the UK on VHS and DVD from BBC Worldwide Publishing. The BBC website has pages devoted to the series at http://www.bbc.co.uk/history/programmes/hob/index.shtml. The three corresponding volumes of Simon Schama's books *A History of Britain* were published by the BBC in 2000–02.

11. *You Are There* is, unsurprisingly, not currently available for purchase in the UK. A radio 'essay' about the series by Walter Cronkite may be found on the NPR website at http://www.npr.org/news/specials/cronkite/. *Culloden* is available for purchase in the UK on VHS and DVD from BFI Video.

12. *War Walks* is not currently available for purchase in the UK. Richard Holmes' books of the two series, *War Walks: From Agincourt to Normandy* and *War Walks 2: From the Battle of Hastings to the Blitz,* were published by BBC Books in 1996 and 1997 respectively.

13. A picture of future trends in television history – including a reference by Bill Jones, Granada's controller of factual programming, to entering 'the pre-archive era' – was given in an article 'Walking with hybrids' by Maggie Brown which appeared in the *Guardian* 'Media' section, 24 November 2003, while this chapter was in the final stages of preparation.

14. *Civilisation* has been available for purchase on VHS by BBC Worldwide Publishing; *The Ascent of Man* is not currently available. The books of the two series were published respectively as Kenneth Clark, *Civilisation: A Personal*

*View*, by BBC Publications and John Murray in 1969 and J. Bronowski, *The Ascent of Man*, by the BBC in 1973.

15. This line of argument is coincidentally the precise point of an advertisement by Getty Images which is running in the issue of the journal *Televisual* (October 2003) current at the time of writing of this chapter. The text for this advertisement reads: 'A woman dreamt that she produced a truly amazing film. She'd had the dream several times, but tonight it was different, she realised parts of the film had already been shot. The woman could now make the budget work harder and smarter than ever before. The team was inspired. When she awoke, she found all that she had dreamt was true.'

16. The Filmoteka Narodowa in Poland has published an English translation of both this work and another essay by Matuszewski, with an introduction by Zbigniew Czeczot-Gawrack, as *A New Source of History/Animated Photography – What It Is, What It Should Be* (Warsaw, 1999). Previous English-language translations of *Une Nouvelle source...* have appeared in the UNESCO journal *Cultures* (Vol. 2, No. 1, 1974, pp. 219–22) and in *Film History* (Vol. 7, 1995, pp. 322–4). UNESCO's translation is available through the 'Screening the Past' web-journal hosted by Latrobe University, Bundoora, Australia, and can be found (with an introduction by William D. Routt) at http://www.latrobe.edu. au/screeningthepast/reruns/mat.html.

17. An excellent general history of the film archive movement, Penelope Houston's *Keepers of the Frame*, was published by the BFI in London in 1994. Stephen Bottomore has investigated the history of the earliest impulses towards film archiving in his essay ' "The Sparkling Surface of the Sea of History": Notes on the Origins of Film Preservation' in *This Film Is Dangerous: A Celebration of Nitrate Film* edited by Roger Smither, published by FIAF, Brussels in 2002.

18. Quoted in Raymond Fielding, *The American Newsreel 1911–1967* (University of Oklahoma Press, 1972), p. 227.

19. Responding to criticism from American isolationists, Will Hays, head of the Motion Picture Producers and Distributors of America and patron of Hollywood's self-censoring 'Hays Code', 'responded by denying that the industry was taking a stand on controversial issues. Newsreels in 1940 contained "factual reports" on national defense subjects in only 16 percent of the cases, he said.... Read from another perspective, Hays' statistics suggested that Hollywood was not paying much attention at all to the rest of the world' (Clayton R. Koppes and Gregory D. Black, *Hollywood Goes to War*, Tauris Parke Paperbacks, London, 2000, p. 20).

20. Also quoted in Raymond Fielding, *op. cit.*, p. 228; my thanks to Luke McKernan for helping me locate this quotation.

21. *The Good War: An Oral History of World War II* is in fact the title of a Pulitzer Prize winning book by Studs Terkel (published by Pantheon Books, 1984).

22. *The Secret War* has been available for purchase on VHS by BBC Worldwide Publishing. The book of the series by Brian Johnson was published by the BBC in 1978.

# 5
# The Adventure of Making
## *The Adventure of English*

*Melvyn Bragg*

The word among producers and directors of television Arts programmes is that writers are the toughest subject. Music can float onto the screen however fussily and mechanically shot; painting, some say, is 'made' for the screen, while cinema and well-filmed extracts from plays inhabit an analogous terrain to that of the small screen which revolutionised leisure and burned itself on the culture in the second half of the twentieth century. But poets? Novelists? All those words, those lines and sentences which ache for a second reading, those stanzas and paragraphs which demand an individual pacing, an intimate, a one-to-one relationship between a page and the intent gaze of the reader – how can words be conducted through those busy tubes? And the answer to that question has always been – with great difficulty or not at all.

I think the evidence contradicts that. Certainly when we have given an hour to a closely-observed documentary about a writer on the South Bank Show we have often come up with programmes which hold their own with appreciations in other media. Films on the work of Seamus Heaney or William Golding, for instance, presented the work at some length (completeness was far simpler of course with the poems) and added thoughtful comments and insights from the writers themselves. Locations, too, seen as relevant words were spoken – Salisbury Cathedral for Golding or the twilight sight of boys playing football for Seamus Heaney – gave another layer of richness as did the very presence of the author, the simple recording of the man with all the information given us by a face, a look, a gesture. I can think of dozens of documentaries made by ITV, the BBC and Channel 4 which tend to contradict the prevailing pessimism about putting writers and their words onto television.

\* \* \*

Yet it persists. And so when I suggested not only that we put words on the screen but we put thousands of words on the screen over eight hours and in chronological order beginning 1,500 years ago and imitating the accent and pronunciation of each successive era, there was a deep breath taken. It helped that I had worked on a series called *The Routes of English* for BBC Radio Four and, with Simon Elmes as producer, made twenty-five half-hour documentaries. But what I proposed was a history and not a series of thematic excavations, which had been the pattern in *Routes of English*. History, thanks largely to Simon Schama and David Starkey and others, has emerged as a welcome subject for television documentaries – but these men are academics and besides their history was grand, even text-book in the sense of appealing television material. The History of England – what could be more sword-clashingly, blood-stirringly engaging than that, save, perhaps, isolated personalities – Elizabeth I, Henry VIII? I am not an academic and the alliterative opacities of *Beowulf*, the intrusions of first Norman and then Paris French, the multiplication of West Indian English dialects do not have the same immediate pull.

Amateurs have done good service to the state of learning in this country over the centuries: from vicarages and schoolrooms, from doctors' surgeries and country houses, men and women untutored by the universities of their day have worked up hobbies and local obsessions into scholarship which has sometimes found favour with later scholars and occasionally made a difference. As an amateur historian given three years square bashing at Oxford more than forty years ago, I could hang onto that. As for the subject? These words. These eight hours of words. Well, I was determined to do it and, to bring the nuts and bolts of television to bear immediately, I had a contract. I had a contract with ITV to do eight 'signature programmes', authored and produced by me, and these were the programmes I wanted to do. David Liddiment, then Director of the ITV Network, accepted with good grace.

The title was the first problem. 'The Story of English' had already been used for a television series and a book by Robert McCrum.[1] 'The Triumph of English' was my first title – after all, we were to follow the story of a fifth-century Germanic dialect spoken by a few tens of thousands to a global language spoken and understood by almost two billion people. This was rejected by academics I respected. What about Chinese? What about Spanish? The word 'triumph' was loaded with triumphalism which was too close for comfort to the least defensible claims of Empire which would not do. 'Adventure' was the compromise and the more I weighed it up, the more useful it became. I could write the story as an adventure – a tale of inauspicious beginnings, near extinction, takeover, suppression, fight back, consolidation, flowering and then an expansion which still goes on with little sign of slowing down. 'Adventure' could legitimate the use of cliffhangers at the end of programmes. It had a dash to it.

The structure of such a series is important in several ways. First, the structuring of the team. I was to continue editing and presenting twenty-two programmes a year for the South Bank Show while continuing *In Our Time*, the radio series, as well as one or two other commitments which thankfully were not, as with the radio and television programmes, deadline driven. It was impossible to set aside sufficient resources to make this series financially freestanding and just as I had to run it alongside other work so had the three producer/directors, Robert Bee, David Thomas and Nigel Wattis, the researchers, the production assistants and the production controllers. This had its drawbacks.

The advantage was that it concentrated our minds and made it even more essential than usual that we wrote and rewrote the script until, in the modest number of days we could afford on location, we wasted no time in the merely hopeful filming, which can be the extravagant bane of documentaries. After the initial two months of preparation (while all involved were working on other projects), each film took about three months. Simon Cherry, the script editor, worked closely with me on the scripts, as did all the producers and researchers, and some of them went through a dozen drafts. We used film crews, cameramen and sound recordists we had worked with before. The same applied to the film editors and production managers. The quality of their work was high and well known to us over years; we could all move quickly together; they were totally reliable and could go through weeks of continuous shooting, short nights, no breaks, too much travel, unhelpful customs officers and glitches. Ten days was the maximum shooting period allowed – it was often less. Time in the cutting room was about six weeks. And although I keep referring to 'film', we shot it all on tape, which is far cheaper.

I had read widely for the radio series but I read more for this and found the general works of David Chrystal as invaluable as the close studies of scholars of the quality of Lynda Mugglestone.[2] Some of those who had appeared in the radio series were invited to give comments on particular passages of the language and Dr Katie Lowe of Glasgow University, who had been very helpful especially on the earlier programmes, was employed as a general sounding board as well as a contributor.

The second real structure is not the external organisation but the ordering of the script. At its most simple – how to tell the story. I wanted it to begin at the beginning and go through the usual chronological hoops. There were suggestions that we should structure it by perching on the end of the second millennium and casting out lines to haul in different centuries as the mood took us. There were suggestions that it had to be interview-driven to give it the academic gravitas thought, rightly, to be essential. And how did a documentary look which was a history not of battles or affairs, very important characters or vivid pomp and circumstance, but of words, their origins, their meanings, their arrivals and departures, the swelling of the word-hoard, the slow slow and then the quick quick of influence, the relationship to Latin and French, the sheer better-if-read-off-the-page richness of it all?

There was also a consideration which might seem over-personal in such a piece, but the idea of 'authoring' a television programme was something I had tried only once or twice before, on a limited scale and with limited success. My job on the South Bank Show, apart from editing and helping to shape the programmes, is to gather material, usually via an interview, which will be spliced in with material gathered by the researcher and the producer to form what we hope is a well-textured profile. Simon Schama and David Starkey are used to lecturing. I am not. Yet it would not work, I thought, unless I wrote it and stood at the heart of it. The cohesion and I hoped the conviction would come from the writer/presenter's own sense of the cohesion of the story, own sense of conviction in its importance.

Each programme, this being broadcast on ITV, consists of three parts of approximately seventeen minutes each. That had to be turned into a strength. Thinking of them as three acts helped. The determination to cover the whole story, from the mid-fifth century until today, meant that we had to drive hard and reach a breakpoint, even a cliffhanger. That seventeen-minute 'act' was helpful. It acted as a powerful aid to selection. And so in Programme 1 we 'covered' the arrival of the Saxons, the displacement of Celtic, the re-emergence of Latin through the Church, the power of *Beowulf*, the effect of the Danish invasion on grammar and vocabulary, the part played by Alfred and the spread of English, the arrival of the Normans, their domination and takeover in Norman French of the upper reaches of communication.

'It was the best of times, it was the worst of times.' Dickens like many authors believed in the clarion call opening. When you know that your film will go out at 10.50 p.m. on a Sunday night and the best you can hope for are a few respectful previews in the broadsheets, then you need all the clarion you can muster. One great ally in all this was Howard Goodall, whose music has ranged from that for *Blackadder* to the Proms. He wrote the music for *The Adventure of English*. His wonderful talent was applied to each section of the films with meticulous care and the directors and I saw sequence after sequence given added urgency or pathos or persuasiveness through the music.

\* \* \*

We opened the series on the rooftop of the London Weekend Building which is on the Thames between the Houses of Parliament and St Paul's Cathedral, opposite the Inns of Court, next to Southwark and the Globe, within walking distance of the British Library – about as central to England, Englishness and the English language as I could get. Twenty-five floors above the capital, at night, was, I felt, the best place to launch the series, especially as the roof is cluttered with dishes and antennae which pick up and send signals in English all over the world, and near the flight path of aeroplanes whose landing instructions, whatever the origin of the flight, are in English. Happily, it is just upstairs from our offices, which meant no costly travel expenditure.

It did not quite work out as I had anticipated. The darkness meant that the definition of the splendid dishes was murky; aircraft stubbornly refused to fly near enough to register; the wind threatened me with an early exit over the parapet. But the carpet of lights below, the shape of St Paul's, the fact and feeling of London allowed me to say:

[vo – voice over, spoken out of vision; ms – midshot; sync – spoken in vision; ls – long shot; cu – close up; GVs – general views;]

| | |
|---|---|
| *Various shots of London skyline at night* | MB (vo) *This is the South Bank in London* |
| ms – MB walks into shot, on LWT roof with London in background. | (sync) Two thousand years ago, if you had heard a human voice here, the language would have been incomprehensible. A thousand years ago, the English language had established its first base camp. Today English circles the globe. It inhabits the air we breathe. What started as a guttural, tribal dialect, seemingly isolated in a small island, is now the language of over a thousand million people around the world. |
| *Opening title sequence* | |
| ms – MB on LWT roof with London in background. | MB (sync) The story of the English language is an extraordinary one. It has the characteristics of a bold and successful |

*Continued*

| | |
|---|---|
| | adventure: tenacity, luck, near extinction on more than one occasion, dazzling flexibility and an extraordinary power to absorb. And it's still going on: new dialects, new Englishes, are evolving all the time, all over the world. |
| ls — helicopter shot of surface of the sea. | (vo) Successive invasions introduced, then threatened to destroy our language. |
| cu — parchment manuscript burning on fire. | Our first programme tells that story. |
| cu — parchment illumination (Bede) burning on fire. | |
| ls — castle chamber with mother singing to child in cradle. | For three hundred years, English was forced underground. Our second programme |
| ls — MB climbing exterior steps at Arundel Castle. Cut to exterior ls of Arundel Castle. | tells how it survived and how it fought back. |
| cu — Bible manuscript. Tilt down. | |
| ls — vaulted roof of cathedral interior. ms — altar boys processing the censer and candles. | Our third programme will tell how the English language took on the power blocs of church and state. |
| ls — exterior of the Globe Theatre. cu — marble bust of Shakespeare. | Our fourth, how it became the language of Shakespeare. |
| GVs of New York | In later programmes, we're going to leave these shores as English did, to tell the story of how, in America, the language of one great empire became the language of another. |
| GVs of the Caribbean | We'll visit the Caribbean, where a whole new flock of English dialects took root. |
| GVs of India | India, where English became a commanding, unifying language in a country of a thousand tongues. |
| GVs of Australia | And Australia, where a confident new English was invented by a people, many of whom had been expelled from their mother country. |
| **Archive 1:** | |
| GVs of East Asian cities (Hong Kong, Tokyo, etc.) | We'll travel through time, too, to explore how English in the twenty-first century |

*Continued*

| | has become the international language of business, the language in which the world's citizens communicate. |
|---|---|
| ms – the dome of St Paul's Cathedral at night, plus other shots of the London skyline at night. | These small islands over the last fifteen hundred years have achieved much that is remarkable. But in my view, England's greatest success story of them all is the English language. |
| ms – MB on LWT roof with London in background | (sync) These programmes are about the words we think in, talk in, write in, sing in – the words that describe the life we live. |

I wanted to boast about the reach of the programme and secured (from previous South Bank Shows) rich footage of America, the West Indies, Australia, India, the Far East – all free. This is technically known as pulling a fast one. Some reviewers pointed out how lavishly budgeted we must have been. The basic idea was simple. To convey my enthusiasm for this project; to convince as many viewers as possible that the journey for them would be worth it, to make it look glamorous and at the same time hold to the seriousness of the enterprise. Even at that late slot, three million people tuned in and enough of them stayed to give us an audience average over the hour of more than two million. The critics were, by and large, warm and encouraging. The audience grew. That opening, the world tour, was meant to be heady, cork popping out of the shaken champagne bottle, the celebration, in fact, before the event. We cut, then, to the flat, rather glum, freezing cold shoreline of Friesland, at dawn, with a man on an empty beach taking a deep breath ready to break the news that the English language came from foreigners, invaders, and from here, this rather unprepossessing spot edging the North Sea.

I had decided as far as possible to adopt the style of the reporter bringing the news straight from the location. This, I think, has a television immediacy. Viewers feel that as they are being shown the essential place, and as the reporter is out there, the report carries authority, it seems more real, and it is News, new. The notion of finding an apt location was central to the unravelling of the narrative and to the texture of the programmes. It was not always easy to find a place as specifically apposite as Terschelling in Friesland or, much later, Shakespeare's classroom, Dr Johnson's house, the home of Gullah speakers in the Deep South, Davy Crockett's American Wild West, or the offices of the O.E.D., but we worked at it, finding the mediaeval library in Merton College to 'represent' John Wycliffe at Oxford, the grounds of Rousham House in

Oxfordshire as a metaphor for the sense of order that eighteenth- and nineteenth-century England tried to bring to the language, the Industrial Museum in Manchester for the Industrial Revolution which introduced so many words to the language, Rochester Castle for the assertion that after 1066 the Norman language dominated all the power centres of the land. That cold, bare beach in Friesland then was a deliberate sign of things to come. Even the shot of the sun rising was not an accident – corny, but intended.

But words were what we had come for and here was the immediate root and route of the language that became English. We were on the island of Terschelling and discovered that Piet Paulusman, the weather man, spoke a language and with an accent as near as we could get to how that seminal Germanic dialect might have sounded in the mouths of those who had gone west in the fifth century at first as mercenaries, then as settlers, finally as conquering invaders. Moreover, when we put up subtitles of Mr Paulusman's words, we could highlight words clearly recognisable to the eye and, by transference, also to the ear. Words such as 'three', 'freeze'.

| | |
|---|---|
| ms – Piet Paulusman presenting weather forecast | Piet Paulusman (sync) En dan, moandei, tiisdei en woansdei: it wurden dagen foar   'op it wetter' |
| | MB (vo) Some of his words might sound familiar, like |
| ms – woman behind bar in café watching TV | 'three' and 'four', 'frost' and 'freeze'. |
| cu – Piet Paulusman presenting weather forecast | Piet Paulusman (sync) In temperatuur sa om en naby de trije of de fjour graden. |
| Subtitles: 'Three or four degrees.'       'No frost – it won't freeze.' | Gjin froast, it sil net frieze. |
| ls – windmill in misty landscape | MB (vo) 'mist' and 'blue'. |
| cu – Piet Paulusman presenting weather forecast | Piet Paulusman (sync) En fierders, de kâns op mist. En dan moarn, en dan mei flink wat sinne. Blau yn'e loft en dat betsjut dat … |
| Subtitles: 'Also, there's a chance of mist.'       And then tomorrow,'       'quite a bit of sun, blue       in the sky.' | |

This, it seemed to me, gave us a beginning which reached out as all serious programmes should try to do. By 'serious' I merely mean programmes, on television and radio, which like the best books, ought to make a double attempt: to retain the integrity of the subject and reach a wider than specialist audience. This has been one of the most heartening discoveries, first on radio and now on television. To restrict it just to the field History (in which I would include the *Adventure of English* series), scholars of the high calibre of Simon Schama and David Starkey have reached out without, I think, short-changing (selecting is a wholly different matter) and been rewarded with grateful audiences in large numbers who turned on because they were interested and stayed watching because they were being informed and at a level which satisfied the appetite for 'the real thing' – knowledge from those who have made it their study to know.

If I can digress here for a paragraph. There is a radio programme which I do on BBC Radio Four at 9.00 a.m. on Thursday mornings which, over the past four years, has specialised exclusively in the discussion of 'academic' subjects with the best academics we could bring to the table. Quantum Physics, String Theory, the idea of Youth, the philosophy of Tolstoy, the theories of Maxwell: a wide range and, often, arcane, discussed by erudite contributors. To the surprise of everyone – not least myself and the contributors – the programme thrives, its 'live' audience reach of 1.7 million which, added to the evening repeat, gives it a listenership on the day of over 2 million, holds its own with other programmes in that morning slot and provokes a substantial correspondence. Part of the reaction is on par with the contributors – confirming, contradicting, usually adding. Part is of the 'I know very little about this but thanks for introducing me to it' variety.

The digression underlines the existence 'out there' in the UK of substantial minorities who want to engage in continuous education, especially through the newer, least intimidating and perhaps one could even use the words most democratic of the media. But the claim for their attention has to be two-pronged and the major terrestrial channels stand in a relationship to their potential audiences which is rather different from the more honed and defined station–audience relationship so long and fruitfully established by Radio Four.

ITV has long been regarded as the People's Channel, and often enough worn the badge with pride. But that channel-description makes you think harder when the subject is going to include Middle English, early Norman and Gullah. Piet Paulusman was important in two respects. He reinforced the theme of 'ordinariness', i.e. this was everyday stuff, the words we spoke, their history, their evolution, their victories and defeats, and we started with the weather, a subject of daily discourse in Britain. Piet's 'English' was intended to give recognition to both the strangeness and the familiarity of the words which announced the beginning of the story we were telling. Secondly he let us move into the sterner stuff which had to be the core of the programme: the word lists. These lists, a feature of the programmes, were often reeled off by me as evidence of the number of recognisable words from early centuries or as evidence of new words brought to the word-hoard by successions of invaders and other influences. For as time went on the story developed many unexpected twists, and not least was the way in which English having been influenced by invaders itself invaded or occupied other countries (India, for example) whose native languages in turn 'invaded' English.

So we had the appropriate location, the sense of News being delivered, the sound and sight of 'English' fifteen hundred years ago, all of which followed a deliberately 'show-biz' trailer-opening, and we were still only four or five minutes into the programme. There was one more factor, certainly as important as the rest and much debated by the team. We decided to put words onto the screen. Not as in subtitles, translating Piet Paulusman or, later, difficult Early and Middle English texts, but the words that 'came in'. I wanted the audience to have the double experience of hearing and seeing. Wherever possible we tried to knit them into the broader historical context.

The best example from Programme 1 was the screening at Rochester Castle of Norman words which had become 'English'. Here we used the great walls of that still impressive ruin to provide the location which illustrated Norman power, and at the same time the backdrop out of which the new words zoomed towards the viewer as I spoke them. They came out of the architecture of power. This was the script:

| | |
|---|---|
| ms – MB on ramparts of Rochester Castle with River Medway in background. | (sync) 'Castle' was one of the first French words to enter the English language. The Normans built a chain of them to impose their rule on the country. |
| Various shots of Rochester Castle keep | (vo) This magnificent castle at Rochester was one of the first to be fortified in stone. |
| Graphics: Drawing of Norman soldier superimposed on keep wall. Still: Brass figure of three soldiers with shields and pointed helmets. ls – tilt up interior of Rochester Castle keep ls – Castle exterior | By blood, the Normans were from the same stock as the Norsemen who'd invaded in earlier centuries, but they no longer spoke a Germanic language, rather what we'd call Old French, which |

*Continued*

Graphics: 'armée', 'archier', 'soudier', 'garison', 'garde'.

had grown from Latin roots. Many of the words they spoke would have been very strange to the English but very quickly became unpleasantly familiar. Our words 'army', 'archer', 'soldier', 'garrison' and 'guard' all come from the conquering Norman French.

ms – MB in gallery of Rochester Castle keep.
Graphics: 'corune', 'trone', 'cort', 'duc', 'baron', 'nobilité', 'païsant', 'vasal', 'servant', 'governer', 'liberté', 'autorité', 'obédience', 'traitre'.

(sync) French was the language that spelled out the architecture of the new social order: 'crown', 'throne' and 'court', 'duke', 'baron' and 'nobility', 'peasant', 'vassal', 'servant'. The word 'govern' comes from French, as do 'liberty', 'authority', 'obedience' and 'traitor'.

Pan around interior of Rochester Castle keep.
Graphics: 'felonie', 'arester', 'warant', 'justise', 'juge', 'jurée'.

(vo) The Normans took the law into their own hands: 'felony', 'arrest', 'warrant', 'justice', 'judge' and 'jury' all come from French.

Pan around Rochester Castle dungeon.
Graphics: 'acuser', 'aquiter', 'sentence', 'condemner', 'prisun', 'gaiole'.

And so do 'accuse', 'acquit', 'sentence', 'condemn', 'prison' and 'gaol'.

ms – MB in front of Rochester Castle keep.

MB (sync) It's been estimated that in the three centuries after the Conquest, around ten thousand French words colonised the English language. They didn't all come in immediately, but the Conquest opened a conduit of French vocabulary that has remained open, on and off, ever since. Today French words are all around us.

We then went on to play with French words in markets and restaurants, but the Castle set the mould. One felicity in that location was that the Castle was being visited by a group of about forty young French students whose interested chatter rang around the old stone walls. We taped some of it and filmed them but the felicity of the moment did not make it to the final cut.

This conjunction of words – the speaking and the seeing and hearing simultaneously – could be added to. When we heard and saw the text of

the seventh-century words of the Lord's Prayer in Old English, it was reinforced by music from Howard Goodall which emphasised its religious
power. His music always helped take these texts through the screen to the
viewers. That original rendering of the Lord's Prayer literally spoke to me
and, on that first transmission, to more than two million people late on
a Sunday night, directly, over thirteen hundred years, bringing together
the past and present of their language. For spoken well, and being known
so well, many of the words seemed almost 'of now' and the others were
taken up by the inner ear, the memory of school or church, I hoped, a
second voice, that of today, keeping pace with the television voice of the
reader. If any one sequence – and one lasting much less than a minute –
could stand in this series for what television could attempt to do – without tricks – to bring the apparently inscrutable past, and one, being
religiously saturated, now alien to an increasing number, then this is it.

* * *

But not all the pieces were yet in place. Piet Paulusman was a useful but
not a sufficient indicator of the way in which a programme with
academic ambitions could try to demonstrate that it was not only for
everyman/woman, it was about them. The greatest contributor to the
language has been Anon. Those who ploughed the fields and scattered,
those who came into the mills and found new words for new machinery, even most of those credited with introducing to the language or
inventing new words would be picking up on foundations put together
by people who have no one name. Or too many.

Take OK, for instance. The derivation of OK, okay, allegedly the most
used word in the world, is a casebook study in the origin of a word. The
theories are so many and so various, so many groups wish to claim it.
At one point I thought that it depended entirely on who you were, as
different ethnic, political and academic groups fight for the ownership
of the number one word. Here are just a few of the more respectable theories, brought together by Mike Todd. There are hundreds more ... .The
Choctaw Indians had the word OKEH which means 'it is so'. There is a
report that Andrew Jackson, during the battle of New Orleans in 1815,
learned this Choctaw word, liked it and used it. Woodrow Wilson also
used it when he approved official papers. Liberia has 'Oke', Burmese has
'hoakeh', and these might have flitted over to America before 1840, by
which time it was in familiar use. Then there are the young bucks in
Boston who enjoyed playing with or tormenting the language. 'ISBD'
was used to mean 'It shall be done' for instance, SP meant 'small

potatoes'. In the *Boston Morning Post*, March 1839, OK was claimed as short for 'all correct', which the young bucks spelled as ORL KORREKT. Which brings it out of Indian hands and back to the descendants of the English. In 1840, Martin van Buren was standing as the Democratic presidential candidate and he acquired the nickname 'Old Kinderhook' (he was born in Kinderhook). In March 1840 the Democrats opened the OK Club in New York based on his nickname.

*The Times* in 1939 claimed it was of Cockney origin – Orl Korrec. The French claimed it came from their sailors who made appointments with American girls 'aux quais' (at the quayside). The Finns have 'oikea' which means correct. *The Times* proposed another theory, that Bills going through the House of Lords had to be approved by Lords Onslow and Kilbracken and each initialled them – O.K. Latinists pointed out that for generations schoolmasters would mark examination papers 'Omnis Korecta', sometimes abbreviated. Shipbuilders marked timber for the outer keel as 'OK Number 1', meaning Outer Keel Number 1. The Scots draw our attention to 'Och aye', of which OK may be an adaptation. The Prussians propose that one of their generals fighting for the American Colonies in the War of Independence would sign his orders O.K. – his initials. The Greeks come up with a magical incantation from the past 'Omega, Khi'. When repeated twice it drives away fleas. The American army suggests that in the Civil War the US War Department bought supplies of crackers from a company called Orrins-Kendall: OK appeared on these boxes and came to stand for good quality ... etc. etc. It can get exhausting. Wise linguists now speak of 'coincidental coinage' which covers all eventualities. OK by me.

But here, in the first third of the first programme, I wanted to bring the language home, colourfully and recognisably, to those who do not think such a programme is 'for them'. Some commentators have cleverly and successfully excised class and its twin, snobbery, from the current catalogue of English or Britishness. It's all over, they say, or it has all changed so much, so very much, that it is no longer meaningful. That is a big debate. For the particular purpose of radio and television programmes, my view is that certain accents, openly privileged assumptions, attitudes, platitudes and gravely accepted fatuities still prevail. They may now be dormant in certain areas of life, but in culture they flourish. I wanted as soon as possible in the film to tell The People, just as, I hope, I had already told the Well-educated and even the Academic, that this was their programme too, their life. In words. We did it, again, through places named by the first Germanic invaders. I wanted people to see how deeply bitten into their life the old word-world was.

Graphic: Southern England with runic texture underneath. Tribal names appear: Kent, Essex, Sussex, Wessex, East Anglia, Mercia, Northumbria.

MB (vo) They had divided into a number of kingdoms: Kent, Sussex, Essex and Wessex, denoting the settlements of southern, eastern and western Saxon tribes; East Anglia, named after the Angles who gave England its name; Mercia in the Midlands. Northumbria in the north.

cu – MB on the ramparts of Pevensey Castle.

MB (sync) Throughout these areas many modern place names come from that settlement, or use the words they brought.
We live with them, we live in them, every day.

Montage of place names ending in -ing, -ton, and -ham, all over various OS map images:

MB (vo) The -ing in modern place names means 'the people of'

Graphic:  'Ealing'
Images:    Still – Ealing Studio poster
Still – 'East of Ealing' book cover
Graphic: 'Dorking'
Images:    Still – Postcard of Dorking
Graphic: 'Worthing'
Images:    Still – Postcard of Worthing
Still – Postcard of Worthing
Graphic: 'Reading'
Images:    Still – Postcard of Reading
               Still – Postcard of Reading
               2 drinks coasters with 1912

*[All this was cut to upbeat, jolly music: an 'Oh I do like to be beside the seaside' sound]*

photos
               Tourist Information leaflet
Graphic: 'Bridlington'
Images:    Still – Poster of Bridlington
               Still – Poster of Bridlington
               Still – Poster of Bridlington
Graphic: 'Wigton'
Images:    Still – Tourist Information
               leaflet
Graphic: 'Taunton'
Images:    Still – Postcard of Taunton
               Still – Postcard of Taunton
Graphic: 'Chessington'
Images    Still – Zoo Circus poster
Graphic: 'Birmingham'
Images:    Still – Civic Centre poster
               Still – Postcard of
               Birmingham

-ton, as in Wigton, where I come from, means 'enclosure' or 'village'.

-ham means 'farm', which might surprise one or two Tottenham supporters.

*Continued*

---

Graphic: 'Grantham'
Images:  Whisky into a Grantham glass
         Still – Postcard of church
         Still – Margaret Thatcher
         Still – Tourist Information leaflet
Graphic: 'Cheltenham'
Images:  Still – Cheltenham Spa poster
         Still – Prospectus for Ladies'
College
Graphic: 'Tottenham'
Images:  Still – Spurs' football programme
         Various shots setting up football
         supporters' sequence:
cu – Spurs flag
ls – mounted police in crowd
ms – crowds and touts
cu – South Stand sign
ls – police outside Corner Pin Pub
mcu – barmaid pulling pint in pub

---

So we went football. We went into a football drinking den of such tribal intensity that had you been wearing a tie coloured red (the shirt colour of Arsenal) you would have been physically confronted. We went to the pub next to the ground of Tottenham Hotspur football club and into a crowd of, largely, young men whose noisy talk could have been misconstrued as latent hooliganism. They were, as are so many football fans, breezy, good-mannered, humorous and tolerant in everything save, at pre-match moments, towards the team which is about to play them. We then cut to a formidable army of young men singing the Tottenham Hotspur war song as they advanced on their pre-match pub and then we cut inside the pub to pry on the conversation. The edited version – of the young men in earnest discussion of their team/tribe's chances was

---

| Various shots of three supporters talking | Fan 1 (sync): Of our strikers, none of them can really finish Armstrong. |
| --- | --- |
| | Fan 2 (sync): We just need some youth and pace really. |
| | MB (vo) Examine the language you use today and you will still find |

*Continued*

| | |
|---|---|
| Various shots of pub customers | hundreds of words from a language over fifteen hundred years old. Key words from the names we give family members to numbers. |
| Various shots of three supporters talking, GVs from inside the pub | Fan 1: I think we'll win 2:1 today. |
| | Fan 2: I'll drink to that. |
| | Fan 1: I live in a West Ham sort of area and I've got a lot of West Ham friends. But for this game we'll be enemies. |
| | Fan 2: Well, the home games, I would go with, well, the guys, we'd meet up from the Top Spurs website, or my daughter to other games. I mean, she's five at the moment, loves it, loves singing the songs, the nice ones anyway. |
| | Fan 3: I was coming with my son, so we just go and get something to eat first, go into the ground, savour the atmosphere and watch the game. There have been a few high scoring games over the years. I think the highest we ever beat them was 6:1. A repeat today wouldn't go amiss. |

From there we cut back to me. I had introduced the sequence from the bar of the pub. Now is the time to reveal that at the time of the shooting of the supporters I was not in the pub. I went on the previous day and we faked it. This was to do with the sound quality and with the amount of information I had to deliver clearly.

| | |
|---|---|
| cu – MB inside Corner Pin Pub in Tottenham | MB (sync) Most of those words were from Old English. Nouns like 'youth', 'son', 'daughter', 'field', 'friend', 'home' and 'ground'. Prepositions like 'in' and 'on', 'into', 'by' and 'from'. 'And' and 'the' are from Old English. All the numbers and verbs like 'drink', 'come' and 'go', 'sing', 'like' and 'love'. |

*Continued*

| | But would those verbs have sounded different all those years ago? In a slightly quieter pub, I asked language expert Katie Lowe. |
| --- | --- |

At this stage in Programme 1, further moves occurred which were also thought through and threaded through the whole series. Dr Katherine Lowe from Glasgow University is an expert on Early and Middle English and I was determined that the programme be stiffened by the best academics we could find.[3] She, as others would do, signalled authority. What I asked her to do on this occasion (she appears in the programmes several times) was first to comment on the workaday conversation of the supporters in the pub. Her answer was perfect for us – at once sympathetic and scholarly.

| cu – Katie Lowe<br>Caption: Dr Katie Lowe<br>　　　University of Glasgow<br><br>Various shots of Katie Lowe in conversation with MB | Katie Lowe (sync) They sound a little different. I mean the Old English for 'son' is 'sunu'. That's not so very different. 'Game' is 'gamen'. 'Ground' is 'grund'. And I notice that Steve says that his daughter loves singing songs. If you said that in Old English it would be 'his dochter luvath tha sange singen'. And you can see that that sounds pretty much like modern English. |
| --- | --- |
| | MB: So in fact you can have a good conversation in Old English? |
| | Katie Lowe: Oh yes, you can indeed. I mean, each, each word I'm saying now is from Old English. |
| | MB: Have you any idea how many words there were swirling around, compared with how many we have now? |
| | Katie Lowe: We think it was in the region of twenty-five thousand words. And compare that with an average desk dictionary which maybe contains something like a hundred thousand words. It sounds pretty small. But if you think about the fact that an averagely educated person would have about ten thousand words in their active vocabulary, there are plenty of words to go round. |

The next move was perhaps taking a risk too far. The impact of the Danes on Germanic grammar had been crucial. It was not all that easy to explain to an audience at, by this time, about 11.05 p.m. To tell you the truth, I hummed and hawed. By comparison, lists of words seemed as palatable as ice cream. Yet I thought I would ask Katie to chance it: she did, selecting with great skill, and it came down to this:

| | |
|---|---|
| Various shots of MB in conversation with Katie Lowe. | Katie Lowe (sync): I think it's true to say that Old Norse affects the English language more than any other, because it actually leads to a re-structuring of the language. Old English formed sentences, not by word order, like we do, but by tacking on endings onto the ends of things, like articles and pronouns and nouns. What happens is that, through contact with a pretty similar language, a lot of these inflectional endings start to lose their distinctive nature. And in fact this is a process we can see happening fairly early on in the Anglo-Saxon period. So the language is prone to do that, but contact with the Norse language speeded it up, gave it a shove towards modernity. |
| | MB: Can you give us a very simple example of that? |
| | Katie Lowe: Yes. Let's take a simple sentence like 'The king gave horses to his men.' |
| Still – Illustration of king and his men. Graphic: 'The king gave horses to his men' 'Se cyning geaf blancan his gumum.' | (vo) That would be something like in English 'Se cyning geaf blancan his gumum.' |
| cu Katie Lowe | (sync) Now in Old English you didn't tend to have a preposition like 'to'. Instead you could have a special ending which kind of meant 'to his men' and that would be an-um ending, and you'd just |
| Still – Illustration of king and his men Graphic: 'The king gave horses to his men' 'Se cyning geaf blancan his gumum.' | (vo) tack that on to the end of the noun for 'man'. So you'd have 'gumum' -um ending. |

*Continued*

| | |
|---|---|
| cu Katie Lowe | (sync) Now, the plural word for 'horse' – you want to say 'gave horses to his men' – would have an 'n' on it, so it would be 'blancan'. Unfortunately, towards the end of the Old English period, we start to see that '-um' ending becoming more and more indistinct |
| Still – Illustration of king and his men<br>Graphic: 'Se cyning geaf blancan his guman.' | (vo) and we see spellings like 'guman' –an, just the same as 'blancan' –an. |
| cu Katie Lowe | (sync) It's obvious that the king is more likely to give horses to his men than men to his horses, but you can see that there's a potential there for difficulties, and so we start to see |
| Still – Illustration of king and his men<br>Graphic: 'Se cyning geaf blancan to his guman.' | (vo) prepositions being used in place of those endings which had become indistinct. |

We kept it in. It was at that point, I believe, that we claimed the right to say that, however selective for the general public we might be, we were also not avoiding the major jumps. English Grammar was our Beecher's Brook.

In historical documentaries there is always the question of dramatic reconstruction. Documentary directors tend to favour the idea because it gives them the opportunity to be drama directors. I'm rarely in favour of it. My prejudice was given substantial assistance by Sue Dunford, who ran all the budgets and pointed out that we could afford very little. Very little worked quite well. To 'see' (in shadow, in the Great Hall at Westminster) the first king of England since Harold Godwinson accept the crown in English, to 'see' film extra cowboys working the cattle in the West, to see and hear fine actors proclaiming the Beatitudes of Tyndale – these were reinforcing moments, and much stronger, I think, for being few and brief.

My objection to dramatisations in documentary is simply that I have rarely seen them work well. There was a recent lavish series of documentaries which mixed the two and the problem was highlighted. You were not with the dramatically portrayed figures long enough to be moved by them or given any insight by their impersonations of 'real' characters, and therefore they were cartoonish. When you came back to documentary techniques the film seemed so much faster and more precise at delivering the information that you wondered why you were wasting so much time waiting in the wings while various bits of ornately, expensively costumed business were being played out in the manner of elaborate illustrations of what was often an essential point. It can be done: this mixing of the genres is a temptation which ought to be yielded to. But it takes a very sophisticated director with, I suspect, considerable resources, to bring it off. For this series, I was quite happy with no more than a brisk dab every now and then.

\*   \*   \*

The limitations in such an exercise are not difficult to discover. Length, length and length are the first three: lack of. That is, if you take on a sweep such as the History of the English Language from AD 500 to AD 2000. You can examine on radio or television minutiae or even a single life with something of the density found in an academic book or a well-stocked book for the general reader. But here, to take one instance, the description of English going 'underground for three hundred years' after 1066, while it has a certain truth, had to be qualified, at much greater length, when I came to write the book that accompanied the series.[4] In the sweep of AD 500 to AD 2000 there was simply not the time for the number of exceptions and contradictions which the book registers: yet the emphatic general point gave us a clarity and an entry to a long and complex period which was of advantage.

The second limitation is a lack of shading and nuance compared with a more leisurely study. It is not that 'television' in itself, like some simplifying ogre, abhors nuance and shading... it was I killed Cock Robin. I was the writer and the editor who wanted to cover a large territory with a sense of discovery and excitement. Although I hope I did not blunt the argument, I could not for instance deploy the many fine distinctions being brought to bear on the Great Vowel Shift. That will have to wait for a more extended essay.

In the television history of more modern, let us say later nineteenth- and twentieth-century events and onwards, you have an increasing store of visual and other resources. Film, of course, and photographs; sound recordings and television items; more letters and documents of a wide variety than ever before; sometimes living witnesses. A feast. This richness means that you can move around more subtly while still respecting the fact that you are attempting to broadcast to a wide, often under-informed public. From Jarrow until almost a thousand years later, you have very little save manuscripts, a few illustrations, places, and a very limited number of authentic period documents. This entails certain responsibilities – not the least of which is to make 'real' a past which is often resistant to exhumation.

However, that was the attempt. It was deeply satisfying even though, or perhaps because, it was the hardest single enterprise I have under-taken in television. We reached a lot of people who were delighted to find out about the springs and coursings of their language. The critics on the whole were generous in helping us on. And now I have had the chance to describe the process for this book!

## Notes

1. TV series transmitted in 1986. Book of the same title by Robert McCrum, Robert MacNeil and William Cran, Faber and Faber and BBC Books, 1986.
2. Lynda Mugglestone is News International Lecturer in Language and Communication, University of Oxford and Fellow in English Language and Literature, Pembroke College, Oxford. She is the author of *Talking Proper: The Rise of Accent as Social Symbol*, Oxford, Clarendon Press, 1995.
3. We used on camera: Dr Kathryn Lowe, Senior Lecturer in English Language, University of Glasgow; Kathryn Duncan-Jones, Fellow of Somerville College, University of Oxford; Professor Hubert Devonish, Department of Language, Linguistics and Philosophy, University of the West Indies; Professor Kate Burridge, School of Languages, Cultures and Linguistics, Monash University, Australia; Dr Jane Stuart-Smith, Lecturer in English Language, University of Glasgow and John Barton and Seamus Heaney. Off-camera we used: Professor Salikoko Mufwene, Distinguished Service Professor, Dept of Linguistics, University of Chicago; Professor David Crystal, honorary professor of Linguistics, University of Wales, Bangor and David Graddol, Open University Centre for Language and Communications.
4. Melvyn Bragg, *The Adventure of English: The Biography of a Language*, Hodder and Stoughton, 2003.

# 6
# How Does Television Enhance History?

*Tristram Hunt*

'Riddled with simple factual errors ... an old-fashioned kings and battles narrative ... does little more than massage the complacency of what he assumes to be a middle-brow audience ...', was how Nicholas Vincent described Simon Schama's history of Britain series in the pages of the *Times Literary Supplement*.[1] The dissection could have referred to any number of television programmes by any number of academics not involved in their production. For that is the alleged crime of TV history: dumbed-down, drum-and-trumpet narratives rehashing the old stories in a conventional idiom for a consumer market. In a medium, it is further suggested, wholly unsuited to a nuanced deciphering of the past and one where the demand for drama, spectacle and 'ground-breaking' discoveries inevitably override subtlety and scholarship.

Despite the barbs, with all the major terrestrial channels, as well as a growing array of satellite, producing ever more varied history scheduling there is now greater programming about the past available than ever before. At the same time, history 'A Level' is flourishing as a course choice while university departments are flooded with applicants. Outside of academia there has emerged a burgeoning magazine, newspaper and radio industry catering for local, genealogical and amateur interest. Meanwhile, the traditional institutional organs of history and heritage – English Heritage, the National Trust, local archaeological and antiquarian groups – are enjoying record membership and now constitute a sizeable element of British civil society. Yet is all this of any worth? Are the history audiences and surrounding panoply a regrettable excrescence – an unhelpful diversion from proper historical inquiry best forgotten and certainly discouraged?

I would like to suggest that the benefits of television history generously outweigh its misdemeanours and taken as a whole the growth in history programming has enhanced understandings of the past. Television history can act as a powerfully beneficial force helping to democratise knowledge, develop new approaches to understanding multiple pasts, and generate instructive public debate about the function and relevance of history. Indeed, television history is now a vital component of how millions of people interact with a past. The question is no longer one of validity but of progress; not whether television history is a good thing, but how do we make it better.

\* \* \*

When it comes to analysing history on the television normally sophisticated critics undergo a collapse in their analytical powers. For television history is not, as many detractors contend, a unitary discipline worthy of unitary disparagement. The medium varies as much as books or radio. A tightly authored series such as David Starkey's *Elizabeth* diverges from the historical journeying of Michael Woods. Such personality-led programmes are themselves markedly different from the more detached, talking-head and narrated series such as Laurence Rees' *Nazis: A Warning from History* which is even more distinct from the reality history shows of *The Edwardian Country House* or *The 1940s House*. In turn, they are clearly distinguishable from the growing crop of historical drama documentaries (such as *Anne Boleyn's Sister* or *Peterloo*) which are obviously separable from archaeology-focused history (*Meet the Ancestors*) or indeed the re-coloured footage of the world wars and the British empire put out by ITV. And let us not forget the arrival of pop cultural history in the form of *I Love 1970/1/2/3 ... ad nauseam.*

As important as an understanding of the breadth of programming is a proper appreciation of the history of television history. Not simply *The Great War* or *The World at War* or even such early 'landmark' productions as *Civilisation* and *The Ascent of Man*, but also challenging series on empire during the 1970s, Ireland in the early 1980s, as well as John Roberts' panoramic if poorly titled *The Triumph of the West*. Meanwhile, Thames, Granada, Central and independent companies such as Flashback, as well as collectives like the Television History Workshop, were producing award-winning and intellectually challenging accounts of the near and far past. The establishment of Channel 4 in 1982 only serving to accelerate a trend for history, and especially social history, programming.

But this vast array of styles, periods and formats seems of little interest to the more blinkered critics. To many faculty pooh-bahs, television history uniformly contains the default sins of superficiality, pap story-telling, overblown drama, and an often wilful refusal to address the complex. This extraordinary lumping together of competing strands of television history would never similarly be applied to the printed text. Rightly, critics realise the range which exists between a PhD thesis, a scholarly monograph, an article for an academic journal, a popular history work, and a newspaper opinion piece. All serve different purposes, engage different audiences, and all contribute to an understanding of history in their own way. But this refusal to appreciate the internal dynamics of television history speaks to one of the most distinctive criticisms of the medium: its failure to be a book.

One of the more doctrinaire conceits amongst guardians of the pure history temple is that real history, proper history, is synonymous with the written word. History, they contend, is created and dispersed only by means of the journal and the book. Those who stray outside the confines of the written word are involved in many things – popularisation, entertainment, even 'edutainment' – but not history as it should be practised. And much of their passion for the printed text holds true. Within the broad acreage of a book, there is indeed greater opportunity to develop arguments and provide contexts more fulsomely, support a thesis more cogently, display a deeper nuance with the topic, and explore contrary analyses. At the same time, the process of research and understanding is developed through the text. Footnotes allow for a lineage of knowledge and an invitation to further scholarship and counter-argument typically unavailable to the viewer.

Yet history has never been solely coterminous with the printed book. As Simon Schama has rightly argued,

> the beginnings of Western history were meant, especially in the hands of Herodotus, as part of the oral, and performative tradition. Beyond the monk-written memorials and muniments, there remained of course a strong, unofficial tradition of performative history; strongest indeed exactly where it reached beyond a small cluster of brethren.[2]

It seems that historians who are so often willing to celebrate the lost customs of oral history and traditions of storytelling are unwilling to accept a modern variant. Through television history and the history of television our society is telling stories about ourselves to ourselves – a concept which is perhaps more easily understandable to sociologists and anthropologists than historians. And the great benefit of television history is that it goes beyond the word to the image.

A defence of television history necessarily involves a belief in the power of imagery as a vehicle for understanding. Across an array of historical disciplines, television can foster an occasionally unrivalled ability to empathise with and appreciate the context for events in the past. Popular understanding of military history, whether it is Max Hastings recalling the events of the Falklands War at Goose Green or Richard Holmes recounting Second World War heroism at El Alamein, has been enormously enhanced by the opportunity for viewers to see the geographical location and appreciate something of the physical conditions facing soldiers on the battlefield. While anyone who has had the pleasure of watching Ken Burns' documentary series on the history of Jazz will know how television can bring social and music history to a wondrous pitch of life. One of my own favourite history programmes is another US social history entitled *Wisconsin Death Trip* which might sound like a trashy horror flick, but is in fact a gripping story of an 1890s Wisconsin mining community made up of Scandinavian émigrés in the midst of an economic downturn and spiritual frenzy. Directed by James Marsh, the film is structured around garish local newspaper reports as well as the macabre still photography of the local morgue. Through a trail of characters and journalistic accounts of the time, the film provides both a powerful account of a nineteenth-century industrial community on the brink of psychological and social breakdown and a historically fascinating portrait of the other side of the American frontier myth.

With its ability to record visually the genealogy of aesthetic influence and now, with modern CGI techniques, to explore the very process of construction, television has also broadened popular understanding of architectural history. The epic BBC1 programme *Pyramid* provided an extraordinary introduction to the physical processes and stylistic development of the Egyptian Great Pyramid, while art history, from *Civilisation* to series by Robert Hughes and Neil MacGregor, has long benefited from the powerful immediacy of visual representation. Historically, television has even allowed for a greater appreciation of visual authority in non-literate societies. John Ruskin famously described St Mark's cathedral in Venice as 'a great Book of Common Prayer; the mosaics were its illuminations, and the common people of the time were taught their Scripture history by means of them ...'.[3] In his *History of Britain* series, Simon Schama gave us a taste of that unknown mental world by recreating the visual architecture of a pre-Reformation church. It was an illuminative leap back into a lost intellectual universe.

Of course, it is modern history which has benefited most obviously from the ability to reproduce archive news footage and call to the bar of history those involved in events. The high-profile interviewees in Jeremy Isaacs' *The World at War* and *The Cold War*, as well as Brian Lapping's brilliant contemporary histories *The Death of Yugoslavia* and *Endgame in Ireland*, offered viewers an unrivalled, personal insight into historical periods and decision-making processes. It also allowed for a welcome plurality of views and cross-section of participants. To hear both Mrs Milosevic and former US Secretary of State Madelaine Albright on the Kosovan–Serbian wars provided a gripping entry into mid-1990s Yugoslavia. Leaving aside objections over inherent structures of bias within directorial agendas, some elements of the past are best brought to light by the ability to hear the words and watch the reactions of first-hand participants to events in question.

But these insights are not limited to wars and treaties, the drum and trumpet. Channel 4 recently aired a masterful documentary on Sikh immigration into post-war Kent, *Sikh Street*, which allowed for a rich piece of social history looking at the cultural interface between Gravesend's tightly-knit, white working-class community and the immigrant arrivals. Gender, race and, through the transformation of terraced housing, even architectural history were explored through eyewitness interviews and telling but detached camera work. Even more dramatically, the power of the on-screen interview was displayed in Laurence Rees' *The Nazis* where the intricate atrocities of the Nazi past were revealed as men and women were faced with their war-time records as murderers or collaborators. Here, dare we say it, television history can prove superior to the written word.

\* \* \*

Yet too few academics see it that way. For opposition towards television history has not in the main emanated from archivists, museum directors, amateur enthusiasts or history publishers – but instead from tenured professionals. Which raises some intriguing questions about the intellectual identity of university historians. British history has always enjoyed a strong tradition of engagement with the public sphere. Leaving aside Carlyle's struggle against Dry-as-dust and the literary histories of Macaulay and Trevelyan, in the post-war ranks of Peter Laslett, Hugh Trevor-Roper, Isaiah Berlin, John Plumb, E.H. Carr, A.J.P. Taylor, Alan Bullock, Kenneth Clark, E.P. Thompson, Eric Hobsbawm and Jacob Bronowski there was a welcome ease with exploring historical controversies within a public context. Carr and Berlin were masterful radio performers; Taylor, Clark and Bullock stand at the font of television history; while Trevor-Roper,

Thompson and Plumb regularly filled the pages of the *Spectator, New Statesman, Listener* and *Saturday Review*. As David Cannadine has remarked, 'Plumb believed that history should be an integral part of the broad national culture of the day.'[4] It is perhaps no surprise that many of today's most gifted public historians – Linda Colley, Niall Ferguson, Norman Stone, the late Roy Porter, Simon Schama and David Cannadine – were supervised at one point in their academic careers by Plumb. And it is even less surprising that one of Plumb's finest essays was on G.M. Trevelyan, a historian who found he could only write away from the abstract interests of Cambridge academia. 'They lacked story; they lacked drama; they lacked the warmth of human life.'[5]

What much of the post-war generation had in common was a shared experience of life and work outside of the university – whether in government, wartime service, or the media. There was less of a precious sanctity about the academy being the alpha and omega of historical inquiry and instead an acceptance of a broader sphere for historical debate. They enjoyed writing and debating in public – none of which seemed to diminish the quality of their scholarship. However, the ensuing decades saw a steady growth in reverence for university history as the arbiter of historical relevance. The increase in faculty numbers and the 1960s centrality of the university to cultural debate ensured its dominance over the historical field. But after a fifty-year hegemony, with the growth of the media, extra-university research institutes, and thanks to large publishing advances the ability of independent historians (such as, for example, David Starkey, Anthony Beevor or John Julius Norwich) to contribute to scholarly debate, it appears the totalising power of the academy might be on the wane. Indeed, the power of the university is starting to look like a phenomenon peculiar to the latter half of the twentieth century.

For some twentieth-century scholars, like E.P. Thompson and then Raphael Samuel who so passionately celebrated the world of 'unofficial knowledge', the study of history outside the strict contours of academic life was a consciously political act: a belief in the democratisation of learning through institutes such as History Workshop, the Open University and the Workers Educational Association. I believe that television at its best can be regarded as a continuation of that process and retains a similar capacity to broaden understandings of history amongst millions who would otherwise remain ignorant. Because of the huge national and international audience which can be reached, well-produced television history has the ability to inspire ever greater numbers about their pasts, empowering them with knowledge and understanding. As Sally Alexander, one of Raphael Samuel's intellectual executors, puts it, 'The dramatis personae, events and images of Britain's past which Schama and others compose have brought charisma and passionate argument to bear on the meanings of that past and possibilities for Britain's future.'[6]

For television history is often only the beginning of a process. The viewer is not always the inert, channel-hopping philistine, but an engaged participant who is initially drawn into a subject by contact through a programme. In what is called, in dreadful parlance, 'a learning journey', the viewer might proceed from a television programme to a channel website to further reading to historic visits and then even to an Open University or higher education course. Certainly in the wake of my own BBC2/Open University series on the English civil war, the Open University received an unprecedented number of enquiries and then take-up of courses on seventeenth-century history. For progressives, the capacity of television history to broaden learning, democratise knowledge and generate public discourse has to be regarded as a laudatory quality.

However, the growing interest in history is not limited to the unofficial realms of knowledge. Figures released by the Universities and Colleges Admissions Service reveal that students applying to read history at university rose by 4.3 per cent in 2003. Today, there are 15,000 sixth-formers taking A Level history, 30,000 undergraduates reading history, 3,000 research students studying for higher degrees and 3,000 university teachers. According to David Cannadine, 'more history is being taught, researched, written and read, and is concerned with a larger part of human experience, and embraces a wider spread of the globe, than ever before'.[7] It would be foolhardy to argue that this is the sole result of television history, but through the numerous conversations I have held with sixth-form tutors, university entrance dons, and students themselves I know television has played a contributory role in helping to increase the discipline's academic popularity.

All of which, one might have thought, would have been welcomed by university academics. But the 2003 annual survey by *History Today* magazine discovered that many lecturers thought television history was, on the contrary, undermining university study by encouraging students to believe the subject was an exercise in storytelling rather than a rigorous intellectual discipline. Karen Sayer, of Trinity All Saints College, Leeds, thought television history reinforced students' 'desires to be told stories rather than acquire the skills of the historian'. Stephen Constantine, senior lecturer in history at Lancaster University, warned that, 'History at university should not be glossy "edutainment" reducing students to passive ciphers.' Others disparaged falling literacy and an increasing cohort of 'not very bright students'. John Charmely, professor at the University of East Anglia, was one of the few to voice a note of caution, suggesting it was 'a little ungrateful of professional historians to bite a hand that is helping to feed them'.[8]

Such criticisms are part of a broader misconception about the function of television history: that it is somehow treading on academic toes and, in so doing, inevitably 'dumbing-down' the discipline. But television history cannot and never should be regarded in the same light as academic research. Its purpose is to excite and inform a broad public, not push the boundaries of scholarship in the same way as a monograph or journal article. Television history is doing its job if it engages general attention and manages to encourage students into the lecture hall or readers into the bookshop – it is then up to academics to nurture a deeper understanding of historical inquiry. Which is why the hostility of many university personnel to television history is so curious for the two are rarely involved in the same project. A history programme is not competing on the same terrain as a book, seminar or lecture. It is purposefully designed for a mass audience, using a judicial edit of sound and vision to make an argument or offer a depiction of aspects of the past.

Academic scholarship is alternatively often involved in highly nuanced, frequently methodological debates about a far more particularised historical controversy. Its audience is limited to others with a developed understanding of the subject and an appreciation of the significance of the polemical interjection. Through a dialectical process of interventions, in books and journals, a greater realisation of the passage of events is meant to be uncovered. Which other, more generalist historians are then able to transplant into a broader narrative. The truly gifted historian is, of course, the scholar able to combine iconoclastic research with the literary skills to produce new findings in an understandable format for the general public. Again, this is most readily achieved through the book rather than the television programme. And it must always be remembered amongst media executives and television historians that it is only because of this hard scholarship that the broad sweep of a series is able to be compiled.

\*　\*　\*

The creation of coherent narratives is one of the lead virtues of television history. The ability of producers and historians to tell important stories about the past to as large an audience as possible while drawing on the latest scholarship must stand as the medium's defining attribute. Kenneth Clark's *Civilisation*, Jacob Bronowski's *The Ascent of Man*, Simon Schama's *History of Britain* all made powerful polemical arguments about a huge range of history managing to marshal the factual analysis in a comprehensible way. Whether one agreed or not with the ideological agenda the programmes nonetheless constituted engaging, authored narratives which engrossed millions of viewers with their historic take. And as such could be regarded as precisely a return to oral traditions of performative history. But when so much academic work is focused on research, with professionals talking to professionals, with scholars less and less keen to place their findings within a broader contextual field, then the engagement with the public is ever more diminished along with respect for 'popularisers' within the academy.

It is a situation which has only deteriorated with the onset of post-modern methodologies. While welcome advances in understanding have been ushered in with the linguistic turn, new approaches to gender and race history, and a proper appreciation of cultural semiotics, too much post-modern history has had the effect of raising an unscaleable intellectual wall between an intelligent public and professional historians. The writing of history to inform or educate the public sphere is arguably a dying art as administrative demands and career pressures for research papers crowd out narrative histories. In its more admirable manifestations, television history could be regarded as a part of the process of bridging the gulf: ensuring the achievements of an all too often introverted academe receive public acknowledgement and an appreciation of their relevance. And it is an increasingly important task in a diminishing public sphere with universities under ever greater pressure to justify their resources. The narrative strengths of television also serve to amend some of the more gaping holes in the education system. Extraordinarily, Britain is the only country in Europe where you can give up learning history at the age of fourteen. While our forward-looking EU partners force their children to study the past in far greater depth, the so-called nostalgia-ridden, heritage-crazed British allow schools to drop the subject after the briefest and most arbitrary of surveys. The predictable result is a disturbing lack of knowledge among the fifteen to twenty-four age group – annually revealed in surveys by the *Encyclopaedia Britannica* on the state of historical awareness.

However, it is not simply a question of Domesday books, Norman invasions, Waterloo and Reform bills; it is a broader psychological condition about contemporaneous living. As Eric Hobsbawm put it in the introduction to his *Age of Extremes,*

> The destruction of the past, or rather of the social mechanisms that
> link one's contemporary experience to that of earlier generations, is
> one of the most characteristic and eerie phenomena of the late twen-
> tieth century. Most young men and women at the century's end grow
> up in a sort of permanent present lacking any organic relation to the
> public past of the times they live in.[9]

A process which in Britain has only been exacerbated by a utilitarian
teaching of history in schools focused more on fostering employable
skills than a coherent idea of the past. So the 'application of numbers',
'working with others', 'improving own learning and performance' [sic]
has more weight than teaching an intelligent narrative of British,
European or global history. The result is a confusingly episodic and disjointed approach to learning where few lessons can be drawn or any
manageable view of the past developed. There is little sense (however
qualified) of a national narrative; no idea of how Britain or Europe have
come to be what they are today.

The consequence of this confusing mêlée of periods combined with
the emphasis on skills rather than narrative and history's peripheral status on the syllabus can be a breakdown in any coherent understanding
of the past. According to one teacher I spoke to specialising in modern
European history, by the time his pupils enter the sixth form 'they have
no concept of agency or change or dynamic in society'. Jumping mer-
rily from the Tudors to the Black Death to Hitler it's barely surprising.
The virtue of television history is that it provides a clear, comprehensible narrative which can be both engaging and informative. Daniel
Power, a lecturer in medieval history at Sheffield, has even suggested
that 'TV history gives them [students] a better sense of the chronological
and geographical breadth of history than A Levels'.[10]

Ironically, given the often superficial and instantaneous nature of the
medium, television history can also help to undermine elements of the
permanent present which Hosbawm identified. The growth in archaeological and architectural television history, the success of local and
genealogical histories, can be attributed to their capacity for helping to
cement the individual within a broader historical lineage. Indeed, in an
era of devolution, globalisation and social transformation that search
for identification – national, familial, racial – is often regarded as one of
the key elements behind the success of television history. Certainly, the

success of Schama's *History of Britain* seemed to speak to a form of *fin de siècle* concern about the nebulous nature of Britishness, while Richard Evans, professor of modern history at the University of Cambridge, sees the enthusiasm as a more specific desire for individual identity in an era lacking traditional class or geographic cohesion. 'What we are has to be seen as the end product of a process of becoming, a process that only history can recount and explain.'[11] A history that is intelligible, narrative driven, and accessible.

*   *   *

Television history can reach millions and in so doing has the capacity to stir wide-ranging debates about identity, heritage, class, religion, race, gender and every other myriad topic which the study of history entails. The pervasive power of the small screen has an effect way in excess of books, newspapers, even lectures. That can obviously be for good or ill, but in the case of much history programming it has encouraged a number of worthwhile and long overdue debates. A good case in point was the recent Channel 4 series, *Empire – How Britain Made the Modern World*, by Niall Ferguson. As Granada had done previously with its own *End of Empire* series, Ferguson's polemical adulation of the British empire managed to encourage the germs of a much needed national discussion about the legacy of Britain's imperial past. Although I disagreed with much of Professor Ferguson's utilitarian critique of empire, the series attracted millions of viewers and opened up an exchange of opinions in the national as well as community press. Aired against the backdrop of American imperial aspirations, it was in my view a highly successful, articulate piece of publicly attuned broadcasting. Partly as a result of Ferguson pushing a debate about empire into civil society, there came a renewed interest in its teaching within schools. The forces of conservatism mobilised, under the banner of the Prince of Wales' summer school, to demand its renewed appreciation within the history syllabus. The ideological agenda behind this campaign can and should be deprecated, but the fact that there existed a debate is to be welcomed. And much of that was down to the opening-up of the subject through television history.

Similar debates came in the wake of Simon Schama's *History of Britain*, my own series on the English civil war, and any number of individual documentaries on controversial topics. Meanwhile TV events such as *Great Britons* or *Restoration* are purposively focused around generating public engagement. Discussion of the past, based around a commonly agreed arena of evidence, is as important to the development of the subject as the research into the past. For history, after all, is driven by interpretation with the subject only truly coming alive when it is actively, passionately debated. When historians are accused of feuding it is a sign of a discipline in rude health. All of which makes the fashion for meaningless, soap opera histories – of bodices, minor aristocrats, and sepia court corridors – the more frustrating. Here is a history which, to paraphrase Blair Worden, invites us 'not to think, not to exercise our imaginations, but to gawp'.[12] Television history at its best invites us to question assumptions, be entertained but also intrigued. Not simply to luxuriate in a Merchant-Ivory glow. As William Camden used approvingly to quote Polybius: 'Take away from history why, how and to what end things have been done, and whether the thing done hath succeeded according to reason; and all that remains will be an idle sport and foolery, than a profitable instruction; and though for the present it may delight, for the future it cannot profit.'[13]

Television history, like any other medium, has its faults. As there are good and bad lecturers, inspiring and dreadful radio programmes, insightful and bland books, so television history ranges from the enlightening to the execrable (see Channel 5's *The Most Evil Men in History*). History on television is not, as Michael Burleigh has argued, merely a 'bubble, ... an illusion used to justify shelling out huge amounts of money'.[14] It has instead become an integral element of the popular historical medium. And while it does not, and can never, occupy the same research terrain as historical journals or academic monographs, history programming does constitute a crucial element of the broader, popular history genre traditionally dominated by civil associations, print and radio. As such, we are entering a new paradigm. The question should no longer be, does TV enhance or diminish history?; it should be, how do we produce the highest quality history programming? The medium should not be discussed *sui generis*, but seen in the same light and subject to the same critical constraints as popular history books and radio programmes. In my mind, the question of validity no longer holds: we are now in the terrain of knowledge-sharing and creative development rather than questioning whether we should be doing this at all.

So, where is there room for improvement? To my mind, one of the most glaring omissions of modern television history is in the field of intellectual history. From Thomas More and Francis Bacon onwards, Britain holds a centripetal position in the history of western political thought. And this culture has been reflected amongst our historians. Part of the greatness of the Anglo-American post-war historical community lay in its ground-breaking work on the history of ideas. From

Peter Laslett to Isaiah Berlin to Quentin Skinner, John Dunne and John Pocock, intellectual history and the history of political thought has provided amongst the most exciting avenues of new research within the academy. Yet very little of this has ever been transferred to a broader audience on TV. While Simon Schama intelligently addressed eighteenth-century conceptions of liberty in his *History of Britain,* and Oxford Films produced an interesting discussion of Machiavelli and his lessons for modern politics in their mid-1990s *Timewatch* programme 'A Memo from Machiavelli', I can think of few recent mainstream programmes dedicated to the history of ideas.

There is an obvious visual difficulty in dealings with esoteric concepts such as equality, the state, utilitarianism or indeed the invisible hand. Part of the challenge I faced in making my programme on Isaac Newton for the *Great Britons* series was explaining the intellectual transformation heralded by the seventeenth-century Newtonian revolution: the move from a pre-modern fear of the natural world to a contention that it was possible both to predict and then control the forces of nature. This constituted a marked shift in the history of ideas. But I like to think we managed it through a mixture of reconstructions of Newton's own life, pieces to camera, rostrum and modern footage explaining the totality of our Newtonian universe. If you can describe that, I don't think it's impossible to take a look at our great works of political thought. Since we must all now consider these texts within their political and social contexts, the story of their development presents the opportunity for some exciting TV history: Hobbes writing the *Leviathan* watching the English civil war unfold exiled in 1650s Paris; Locke and the turmoil of late Stuart London and the history of the exclusion crises; More and his precarious place in the Henrician court; John Stuart Mill and how his tortured childhood and complicated emotional life moulded his concept of personal liberty. All gripping stories carrying vital intellectual relevance.

Similarly, I would argue for more social history. The kind of intimate, enigmatic but nonetheless revealing moments of the historical past of the kind Eamonn Duffy brought to life in his *Morebath* – a wonderful account of a Reformation village which can be read in the same intellectual lineage as Emmanuel le Roy Laudurie's *Montaillou.* Both rich works illuminating lost cultures through an artful mix of drama, pathos and intriguing personages. More of this kind of history should be transferred to TV. The *Plague* and *Fire* films on Channel 4's recent seventeenth-century series showed precisely how it can be done as each provided nuanced stories of the Black Death and the Great Fire using parish records. The brutal intimacy of the analysis made the programmes all the more real and events more terrible. However, while television history is inevitably drawn to the personal and the iconic, there is also room for some television rendering of the kind of social forces which underpin historical developments. While few producers would be given the resources to film a Braudel-style account of nature, man and land, too much television history emphasises the fickleness of personality as the sole driver of events. In the case of Henry VIII, Anne Boleyn and the Reformation, there is arguably a case for this. But shouldn't we also learn about Lollardy, growing trade links with the Dutch, rising literacy, and other causational factors? Broader social, intellectual and economic currents need to be given an airing. Although whether Ian Kershaw's brave demand for a history of bureaucracy will be taken up appears less certain.[15]

Equally, I hope television history now has the confidence to stray outside of the national narratives and maybe even beyond Europe to the developing world. TV executives once took a chance with commissioning lengthy histories of Britain and the same ambition now needs to be demonstrated if the genre is going to develop beyond repeating stories about ourselves. As Peter Mandler has rightly argued, history is not simply about bolstering a certain sense of national identity more often than not premised upon continuity rather than change. It can and must, in a public sphere, offer alternative rationales.[16] Television history has a profound power to generate a general public reassessment of traditional narratives and prejudices grounded in certain historical readings. This has to be deployed intelligently and creatively, taking modern scholarship to look afresh at comfortable renditions of the past. But it needs to extend beyond the instinctive television desire to uncover the 'real', revisionary truth behind iconic events and individuals and develop something more sophisticated than a cynical rubbishing. Meanwhile the ceaseless and ultimately barren quest for three million viewers means that such provocative programming is all too frequently bypassed in favour of a familiar recitation of Nazis, Egyptians and SAS 'revelations'.

It was the bewitching flow of their language which attracted such a vast readership to the histories of Macaulay, Carlyle, Green and Trevelyan. Amidst the search for a new visual literacy amongst historians, we should not lose sight of the value of language. The crime of so many television-history programmes is as much to do with the poverty of script-writing (with words hide-bound by pictures too often written by media studies producers) as the camera-work or editing. It is the primary task of historians involved with television programmes, as I have learnt the hard way, to assume as much editorial control as possible within a working relationship premised on trust with the director/ producer. Far too often the pictures can lead the words in highly uncomfortable and even misleading directions. It is when the visual comes overly to dictate the programme structure and interpretation that television history falls down. But we should also not forget that the relationship with television remains relatively new and given that, some five hundred years in, historians are still at war with their publishers, the historian–producer relationship has a long way to mature.

*  *  *

Like the printed word, the audio-visual history is here to stay. Sometimes complementing, often infuriating, the world of university scholarship, it takes its place as a fundamental component of the popular historical landscape. As with the blandest textbooks or dullest lecturers, it will have its weak spots, but it can also shine with the finest of its audio or literary rivals. If one believes that more people studying history, debating history, reading history and visiting historic sites are signs of a vigorous intellectual engagement with the past, signs of enhanced understandings of multiple pasts, then television history should be nurtured encouragingly rather than dismissed ignorantly.

## Notes

1. Quoted in David Herman, 'Cabbages and Kings', *Prospect*, April 2002.
2. See ch. 2, this volume, p. 24.
3. E.T. Cook and A. Wedderburn (eds), *The Collected Works of John Ruskin*, London, 1903, X, pp. 129–30.
4. *History Today* (2002), 52, 2, p. 27.
5. J.H. Plumb, *Men and Places*, Penguin, 1966, p. 253.
6. *Guardian*, 21 July 2003.
7. David Cannadine, 'What is History Now?', in J.S. Morrill (ed.), *The Promotion of Knowledge, Proceedings of the British Academy*, cxxii (2004), pp. 38–9.
8. *Guardian*, 21 July 2003.
9. Eric Hobsbawm, *Age of Extremes*, Abacus, 1994, p. 3.
10. *Guardian*, 21 July 2003.
11. Richard Evans, 'How History Became Popular Again', *New Statesman*, 12 February 2001.
12. Blair Worden, 'Do We Get the History We Deserve?', *Sunday Telegraph*, 27 May 2001.
13. William Camden, *The History of the Most Renowned and Victorious Princess Elizabeth, Late Queen of England*. Edited and with an introduction by Wallace T. MacCaffrey, Chicago, 1970, p. 6.
14. Michael Burleigh, 'The End of History is Nigh', *Sunday Times*, 25 August 2002.
15. See, ch. 8 this volume, p. 122.
16. See Peter Mandler, *History and National Life*, Profile, 2002.

# 7
# Hacks and Scholars: Allies of a Kind

*Max Hastings*

All of the contributors to this book are in the business of gathering and disseminating information. This purpose may be modified or diluted in some degree, at my end of the trade anyway, by a requirement to sweeten the pill, to provide 'a spoonful of sugar for the bird', to entertain as well as inform. At one extreme of the spectrum, the task of interpreting history for the media may mean writing a handsomely rewarded 2,000-word article for the *Daily Mail*, as I did the other day, on the theme: 'why are history's great men so often four-letter men?' I am not ashamed of what I wrote, but nor would I claim that writing of this kind represents any attempt upon the higher peaks of culture. The most that can be said of it is that it distributes modest crumbs of historical knowledge at tables where otherwise the past remains a very misty, remote place.

Work of this kind is, of course, incomparably easier than that which takes place at the other, scholarly end of the business, where a researcher might devote months to archival research, eventually to generate an essay for a learned journal on land tenure in Worcestershire in the fourteenth century, which will be read by fewer than a hundred people. I suspect that even the most devoted seekers after truth among us will concede that such pieces can make arid, if not outright dreary reading. But the process of primary research holds pride of place at the head of the river. If it did not take place, if academic researchers were not out there doing the work that many miles downstream, my colleagues and I will gather flotsam from, there would be no history to be popularised by the media.

\* \* \*

There always has been, and always will be, mutual jealousy between hacks and scholars – it is well attested in the literature of ancient Athens and Rome. Many journalists would like to have been scholars, if they had been willing to accept the terms – working without benefit of fame for very modest financial rewards. Myself, I have always been a little haunted by a scene in Tom Stoppard's play *Night & Day*, in which Diana Rigg's character castigates a hoary old foreign correspondent, played by John Thaw. 'Journalists always think they're just doing a bit of reporting to pay the mortgage till they get down to writing the great novel, the big book, the blockbuster history', she says. 'What's so pathetic is that in reality they are doing *the best work of which they are capable.*' It is a reflection of the impact these lines made on me, that I can recite them from memory twenty years after seeing the play. Like many journalists, I have always had an uneasy notion that Diana Rigg may have been right.

Many academics, by contrast, daydream about what wonderful television presenters they would make, if only they did not possess too much integrity to abandon their research and compromise their standards. I was taught at school by a very clever young historian, whose devotion to his craft I greatly admired. Afterwards, when I was working for the BBC, he enlisted my help to get him an audition as a presenter. He got the job, dumped teaching, and spent the next decade trying to become famous. So much for my schoolboy delusions about academic commitment, though this particular teacher eventually saw the error of his media ways and later wrote several brilliant historical studies.

Journalists, who are often well-educated and sometimes even quite intelligent people, yearn for the intellectual respectability of the academics holding tenure. As an editor, proud of employing several hundred clever young men and women, when I read the paper each morning I found it difficult not to ask myself how the results of their labours could so often seem so much less than the sum of their parts. Yet newspaper offices are also often crowded with visiting academics, hankering for the cash and mass audience available to those who can turn out a plausible leader page article. I have never forgotten Niall Ferguson, as a young Cambridge don aspiring to write for the *Daily Telegraph*, telling me that he wanted to be the A.J.P. Taylor *de nos jours*. A by-blow of this ambition was that it took us years to persuade him that it was not necessary to mention Bismarck and Metternich in every piece he wrote, in order to fulfil it.

I have some experience of writing military history books, of making television programmes, of reporting for newspapers. It should console scholars, that there is such a powerful inverse relationship between the breadth of reach a given medium offers, and the penetration of its content to the audience. In the days when I worked full time in television, people often came up to me in the street and said 'I saw you on the telly last night.' But they seldom had the smallest idea what I had been talking about, nor indeed what country I had been reporting from. Recognition was high, but understanding was low. Television is a brilliant medium of impression. It is a much less satisfactory medium of analysis.

Things get a little better, if one writes a newspaper article. If somebody says he has read a piece in the *Daily Telegraph*, on a good day 30 per cent of its sentiments will have got across, though I should add that even at a paper like the *Telegraph*, only about a third of the total readership makes any attempt to read the leader page or the serious features. There is a much better chance of a plausible dialogue with a reader, if one writes a book or contributes to a scholarly publication. If somebody can be bothered to buy the book or subscribe to the magazine, there is a fair chance they will read it. What historical evidence can I offer, to justify these assertions? The anecdotal testimony of correspondence. I am often impressed by the sensible, well-argued comments of people who write letters, whether friendly or otherwise, about books one has written. By contrast, most readers who write letters to newspapers are plainly deranged, and indeed often give addresses of secure accommodation, even prisons. People who watch television scarcely seem able to compose letters at all. If they write to presenters it is usually to solicit help in solving domestic problems relating to their husbands or cats. I jest a little, but all of you with personal experience will recognise something of what I am saying.

The first job I ever had, in my gap year after leaving school, was as a researcher on the BBC's twenty-six-part series, *The Great War*, back in 1963, at the age of seventeen. The programmes were made in the days when BBC factual television was astonishingly well-funded, and when programme-makers still possessed amazingly ambitious ideas about the seriousness of the message they might hope to convey to viewers. Working on the project, albeit as its humblest link, taught me something about the First World War, and rather more about the manic intrigues and serial bonking which characterise life in television, or at least did so in those days. *The Great War* was written by an exceptionally able group of young military historians, which included John Terraine, Correlli Barnett, Alastair Horne and Barrie Pitt. The internecine strife between them would have commanded admiration among the Borgias, but the quality of their broadcast work was very high. I still have somewhere a copy of the lecture all the researchers and writers were given at the outset of the two-year project, by Antony Jay, even then a highly literate television veteran, about the nature of writing for the screen.

The key point Tony Jay made, as valid now as then, was that television is a visual medium, in which it is essential that the words follow the pictures, rather than the other way around. This is a painful lesson for many writers. Most of us have to learn it by experience. That is to say, when we make our first essays in composing television scripts, we write down what we want to say, and then seek to persuade the producer by guile or main force to lay pictures in the wake of our words. This approach is, almost invariably, a failure. The pictures are merely being used as what the trade calls 'wallpaper'. We have to learn to accept that if a viewer retains a memory of any television programme, it is almost invariably a visual one – of an image which has caught his or her imagination – not of a phrase. That is not to say, of course, that the words do not matter, but merely that one must have a clear sense of the thrust of the medium.

Finding visual images for historical programmes, other than for the last half-century, is a difficult task. Much of the archive footage used for *The Great War* was faked. That is to say, in 1914–18 when movie cameras were primitive, it was technically almost impossible to shoot the reality of battle, and therefore scenes shot for contemporary newsreels were almost all filmed during training. Some of the air war sequences used in the BBC series were shot for feature films of the period. I would defend this breach of integrity, as some professionals would call it, on the basis that the visual images possess a broad historical validity, so long as no attempt is made to delude the viewer about their limitations. As an aside, it is remarkable how little war footage shot throughout the twentieth century does, in reality, reflect exactly what it purports to. An immense amount of film of Vietnam shows people shooting at each other, but not infrequently the soldiers were firing their weapons at the request of the cameraman, not in response to the enemy. Like everyone who worked in Vietnam or other modern war zones, I have often seen this done. There is seldom a crib in today's libraries for historical documentary-makers, to alert them to what is authentic and what is not.

Most writers making their first essays in historical television documentary-making try to cram far too many words into the available screen time, in their eagerness to convey the nuances of the story. The result is that we overload both the pictures and the viewers, who will almost certainly be receiving our message at home in the evening after work, a time when their receptivity to complex intellectual signals is at its lowest ebb. The average half-hour television programme contains around four thousand words, many of which merely describe the pictures on the screen. It is a frequent source of frustration for writers who work in television, to discover how little it is possible to say on a big theme in four thousand words. Sixteen years ago, I wrote a book about the Korean War which was 150,000 words long. I then made a four-part television series for BBC based upon it, which contained about 25,000 words, many of which were those of interviewees. I still blush to remember how little information, and what fantastic simplifications, the series contained. That was partly a reflection upon my own limitations, but also I think upon the nature of television.

*  *  *

I have been out filming today for a Channel 4 series on Churchill and his generals. I won't venture to predict that this will be an improvement on the Korean War programmes, but I hope I have learned a little bit about the need to work with the medium, rather than to try to fight it. The only way to make successful television programmes is to develop a limited number of relatively simple thoughts. It is also fundamental to all mass media, television and newspapers, that the thrust of a pro-gramme or article must be about people, rather than about things. It is only possible to rehearse arguments about abstract issues on television or in daily papers by telling a human story. To some scholars, this is a compromise too far, a betrayal too many. But it is fundamental to the nature of the business. If you want to sell history to the media, it must be crafted to fit its requirements. The commonest reason that I found myself, as a newspaper editor, rejecting articles offered by academics was that they could not accept the need to adjust their arguments so as to persuade a mass audience to read them.

History is 'hot' in television just now, but you don't need me to tell you that this means popular history. I was talking recently to a producer who has been working on a new series of programmes about the First World War. I asked him if he had looked at *The Great War* series. He said he had. I asked if he agreed that the scripts were unusually intelligent – I went back and looked at some of the programmes myself recently. Yes, he said, they were pretty heavy stuff. He added: 'Of course, you couldn't possibly get away with scripts like that nowadays.'

It always seem unfair, the degree to which television as a medium favours hams, whether as presenters or witnesses. Thirty years ago, I was filming for a BBC current affairs programme in East Pakistan after a cyclone. We were shooting interviews with survivors and came across one old man who spoke fair English, because he had been a policeman in the days of the Raj. He exploded into a storm of emotion as soon as the camera started running. 'Once I was a rich man, now I am a street beggar!', he shrieked. After a couple of minutes of this, I threw down the microphone in disgust and told the cameraman to cut. 'What did you do that for?', demanded the producer crossly. 'He's great.' 'Oh come on Bill,' I said, 'he's just an old phoney'. 'No, no,' said Bill, 'keep turning'. And so we did. When that film was transmitted, we received a herogram from the office which highlighted our emotional veteran: 'Loved your street beggar stop. Wonderful colour love Peter.' That's the way television always has been, and always will be.

Yet most of us who have the chance to do so seize the opportunity to broadcast, and leap at the chance to make programmes about history, because whatever compromises television enforces, we find the reach of the medium irresistible. It is an intoxicating thing, to be given the opportunity to tell a story to an audience of millions, when one knows that as the author of a book, one is lucky to be able to number its readership in tens of thousands. Don't listen to any broadcast presenter who says that he finds the whole business a bore. Almost all of us who do it, deep in our hammy hearts, love every moment of it. We realise that we can make ourselves identifiable to a vastly wider public through the screen than through even the most successful work for the printed page. We know that we will sell far, far more copies of the next book we write, if prospective readers have seen us on the screen. Contrary to popular myth, television does not pay well, unless one is Cilla Black. Factual television is absurdly poorly financed, compared with light entertainment or sport. The commonest question a television company is likely to ask the presenter of a factual programme is: 'Do you mind flying from Stansted?'

Yet there is never the slightest danger of a shortage of journalists or academics happy to accept almost any terms television offers, to reach that vast audience. In our defence, we might suggest that Macaulay or Trevelyan would surely have taken the same view, as indeed would have the Messiah. I am sure many of you will remember the story of the fuss back in 1938, when J.E. Neale published his biography of Elizabeth. It was one of the first books written by an academic holding tenure which was published without footnotes. In an Oxford common room the bitter cry went up: 'He has sold the pass!', to which a gloomy donnish voice added: 'He has also sold twenty thousand copies.' It was ever thus.

The important thing about television is to recognise its virtues and its limitations without condescension. If it enables millions of people to discover fragments of history that would otherwise pass them by completely, as of course it does, then it performs a valuable service.

A year or two ago, I read a witheringly scornful denunciation of Simon Schama in the *Times Literary Supplement*, by an academic holding tenure at a provincial university. The review was written with an anger and contempt that seemed wholly disproportionate, and indeed explicable only by the reviewer's jealousy. The trade of history is surely in Schama's debt, for opening up the market in a remarkable fashion. If even a few thousand viewers move on from watching Schama paint his broad brush strokes on a huge canvas to read a dollop of heavyweight history on some specialist period that has caught their fancy, then the whole exercise is justified. The purpose of everything all of us do, at our different levels, is to stimulate curiosity. John Lewis Gaddis has observed that even the greatest academic historians cannot hope to depict the past, because it is so vast, and so much of it is inevitably unknown to us. They can aspire only to represent the past. Television may do this impressionistically rather than analytically, but if it is done well, the representation will possess huge power for all manner of people who will never read Steven Runciman or Hugh Trevor-Roper.

Scholars and journalists have it in common, that to justify writing a book or a newspaper article or a television script, it is necessary to convince a publisher that one has something new to say. This claim is just as often spurious when the author is a veteran fellow selling his wares to a university press, as when he is a journalist contributing to the BBC or the *Daily Mail*. I have always liked a line in Boswell about Oliver Goldsmith: 'When Goldsmith began to write, he determined to commit to paper nothing but what was new; but he afterwards found that what was new was generally false, and from that time he was no longer solicitous after novelty.'

All of us will sympathise with Goldsmith's sentiments. When I was editing the *Daily Telegraph*, I banned the use of the word 'exclusive', on the grounds that no story in the British media carrying that tag ever proves to be both new and true. Much the same is true about alleged historical revelations in the media. It is very seldom that an article or a programme unveils information genuinely unknown to scholars. What happens is that a new generation of editors or television producers rediscovers facts hitherto unknown not to science or academe, but to themselves. My first literary agent observed that one can write anybody's biography every ten years. He made that remark thirty-five years ago. Today, that timescale has been dramatically shortened, and the principle applies as much to history as to biography. New books on a given historical event crowd in upon each other at intervals of a few years, with a special impetus provided by anniversaries, which can be registered with any television company or newspaper on a five-year cycle. This is especially true of the field in which I chiefly practise, the Second World War.

*   *   *

Paradoxically, while the media is dominated by neophilia, a desire to profess to discover new evidence – often spurious – on the big issues my trade is most comfortable with familiar legend. I am intrigued by the manner in which the media doggedly sticks with certain historical lines about the war, even after generations of researchers and historians have demonstrated their falsity. For instance, the media takes a relentlessly chauvinistic view about the scale of British achievement in the Battle of Britain. Of course the RAF's stand against the Luftwaffe in 1940 was important, and of course the RAF did well. But the Luftwaffe moved east in 1941 not because it had been destroyed or defeated, but because Hitler's principal ambitions lay in Russia, where they had always been, and not in Britain, which he correctly perceived as impotent to challenge his ambitions on the continent. Likewise, many Second World War scholars have argued convincingly that the British airborne assault on Arnhem in September 1944 could never have succeeded in its objective of bringing about a quick end to the war. But the legend of the 'bridge too far', of a vast opportunity lost in a few days of mishaps on the battlefield, exercises such a powerful magic that it is all but indestructible, and is religiously recycled in every anniversary year with a four in it.

I found myself debating on television recently with a German writer named Jorge Friedrich, who has written a book suggesting that the British are still deeply unwilling to examine their own breaches of the laws of war between 1939 and 1945, even while the British media indulges in constant eager examinations of Germany's. He is quite right about this, of course. Ludovic Kennedy was bitterly criticised in the British media when he wrote a long and painstakingly accurate article about an incident in the Mediterranean in 1942, when a British submarine commander named Skip Myers systematically machine-gunned in the water several hundred German survivors from sunken caiques. Myers was subsequently awarded a VC and died an admiral and a hero, while if he had been a German U-boat commander there is little doubt that he would have been hanged in 1945 for what he did. I remember what a shock it was to me, when I began writing about the war twenty-five years ago, to discover that allied troops quite often shot prisoners, a practice I had been brought up to suppose was exclusively the privilege of German SS men.

I don't here want to get into issues of wartime morality – I am simply making a point about the lingering chauvinism of British media treatment of recent history. It is not that I am a debunker – I enjoy as much as any writer, being able to describe how my own people, the British, did some things rather well, as for example in the Falklands war. But I am intrigued by the manner in which media sentiment about the Second World War, in particular, continues to run on familiar railway lines.

There is an odd contrast here with the First World War. Round about 1930, a view evolved in Britain, warmly encouraged by the war poets such as Graves and Sassoon, that the war had been a terrible mess for which everybody shared guilt. Many modern scholars, including some distinguished German ones, have challenged and indeed discredited this view. Of course there is general agreement that the conflict was a human catastrophe, characterised by immense military folly. But it is much more debatable whether it is justifiable to assert that the allied cause was not worth fighting for. Some good historians have produced a convincing thesis that the Kaiser's Germany was an aggressive military dictatorship, which bore overwhelming responsibility for the outbreak of war in 1914, and that a German victory would have been catastrophic for European freedom. Again, I am not seeking here to debate the merits of the argument – merely to suggest that it is interesting how reluctant is media and popular opinion in Britain to revise the seventy-year-old Graves–Sassoon verdict on the war as a pointless exercise in mutual destruction.

Probably the greatest growth industry in our field in our lifetimes has been that of oral history. I never cease to be amazed by the scale on which, all over the western world, both amateur and professional historians are trawling the ranks of old people, interviewing them on tape about their experiences in war and peace. Vast archives are being assembled in tens of thousands of communities on both sides of the Atlantic. I use oral testimony myself, and this year have seen more than one hundred and fifty survivors in Britain and Germany, Russia and Holland and America, for a book I am writing on the last months of the Second World War. It is a tremendously valuable exercise, for helping one to understand what it was like to do things which are unrecorded in any documentary archive, especially the minutiae of contemporary experience, which a whole generation took too much for granted to trouble to write down. I am especially impressed by what one can learn about the experience of women, which is fascinating and far less fully documented than that of men.

The value of oral evidence seems greater, if one accepts that the legitimacy of documentary evidence can readily be overdone. I remember the wartime scientist Solly Zuckerman telling me that when he went back to the archives to research for his autobiography wartime meetings which he had attended, he was amazed by how little co-relation he discovered between the records and his own memory of what took place. He concluded that the records reflected merely the personal prejudices of whoever was responsible for taking the minutes. It is not that Zuckerman's memory is likely to have been inherently more reliable than those minutes, merely that it is valuable to weigh the two against each other. It is foolish to accord to the written record an excessive validity, which is why all historical writing, even the most scholarly, represents a lunge towards truth, albeit sometimes an inspired one. Talking at first hand to people helps one to grasp a simple but critical truth, that very few of those who take part in great events reflect at all about great questions – the fate of the Jews, the future of Europe. They can relate only to what happened within their own tiny compass.

Oral testimony is especially valuable when dealing with, for instance, Russian and German experience, for which documentary evidence is both thin and unreliable. But it seems essential for any serious historical researcher also to acknowledge its limitations, in a fashion the media often does not. People recounting their experiences sometimes lie, more often drastically edit, their stories. This is especially true, I have found, in dealing with Russians and Germans, who carry so much complex and uncomfortable moral baggage. The Russians, in particular, have no modern tradition of cherishing a search for objective truth. As they get older, so too of course they simply forget things. Their narratives cease to represent a continuous motion picture of what happened to them, and become a random collection of disjointed, blurred still photographs. Conversations with men and women in their eighties do not lose their fascination, but certainly forfeit any claim to be treated as gospel. It seems dismaying that some writers seem reluctant to recognise this commonplace. One of the worst vices of the post-Diana media and social world is the retreat from intellectual rigour, the mounting belief that what someone says they feel possesses a validity as evidence as great as an objective fact. A while ago I heard John Keegan observe that he had spent his entire formative years being educated to believe that the highest virtue was the pursuit of objective truth based upon evidence, and that he found it bewildering and dismaying now to perceive a climate of public opinion in which expressions of emotive sentiment are regarded as deserving of equal weight in an argument with historical facts.

It is a frequent vice of my trade, in discussing contemporary history, to concede an inherent virtue to the testimony of survivors, merely because they are still alive and venerable and can speak, which objectively their evidence does not deserve. It is even highly doubtful whether what a man or woman tells an interviewer in 2002 was his or her state of mind sixty years ago can be relied upon. I feel far more comfortable using oral testimony in a book, in which I can readily load my own view of its plausibility, rather than merely giving air time on camera to a witness, who can so often defraud the audience as effectively as the street beggar I met in East Pakistan in 1972, and whom I referred to above.

\*   \*   \*

Yet we all recognise that one reason the Second World War is such big business for television is that its survivors do still exist to be interviewed for television. The greatest difficulty in projecting earlier history on screen is the lack of visual material to illustrate it. Simon Schama's recent series used dramatic reconstructions. It has become highly fashionable to make programmes in which modern actors or volunteers live out some aspect of historical experience for the cameras, whether as Roman legionaries or infantrymen in the trenches of 1917 Flanders. But the absence of authentic moving pictures remains a huge obstacle in the path of making pre-twentieth-century documentary history programmes. When the attempt is made, however worthy, it is depressing how often the outcome is tedious. The visual difficulties have defeated the film-makers. At the most basic level, it is daunting that no reliable portraits exist, for us to know confidently what any English king looked like, before Henry VII. The Middle Ages, especially, defy the attention of even the most innovative producers, save in the simple aspect of knights in armour. For a mass audience, it is all but indispensable to enlist the service of such colourful images.

I was lucky enough to be taught history at school by some very clever people, including Christopher Thorne, who was later Professor of International Relations at the University of Sussex. They inspired in me and some of my contemporaries a fascination with the subject which has persisted all our lives. We studied history at a time when much of the syllabus focused upon British triumphs on the battlefield over lesser races such as the French, and wholly absorbing it was. A few years ago when my daughter lamented to me the tedium of history A Level, I was unsympathetic until I found that she was being asked to spend much of her time studying nineteenth-century Poor Law, and was invited to write essays empathising with peasants who were having a hard time in the Agricultural Revolution. On those terms, I am amazed that any schoolchild still chooses history at all. I come from a more brutish tradition. Why, today, after a lapse of forty years, can I still vividly remember the Statute of Quo Warranto? Because at school we were told the story of Earl Warenne, who when challenged to prove by what right he held his lands, drew and waved aloft his rusty sword. The teacher who captured our imagination by telling us that story would today, I am sure, be a highly successful presenter for the History Channel. Only by such homely devices have children through the ages, or television viewers in our own times, been persuaded to perceive the charm of the past.

C.V. Wedgwood is today an unfashionable historian, but she brought the seventeenth century to life for a generation of students, in a fashion for which many of us remain hugely grateful. Her word portrait of Stuart England in the first chapter of the King's Peace still makes peerless reading, even if the critics are right about its indifferent sociology. Would that some modern historians whose scholarship is undoubtedly impeccable possessed her literary gifts, her ability to capture a sweep of history. The mania for specialisation among modern academic historians often seems the sworn enemy of accessibility. I am a professional writer and an amateur historian. I have access to a wider audience than most professional historians, because I am a populist. I would like to hope that does not mean I accept a lower standard of proof than academics, but I paint upon less ambitious canvases and I sometimes succumb to the necessity to make generalisations or unqualified assertions that as a student would secure me a mauling from any university tutor. As a writer of books, however, I possess one notable advantage over most academics: because I can get relatively large cash advances from publishers, I am able to spend a lot of money on research, especially abroad, and I would like to hope that this shows in the outcome.

The treatment of history by newspapers and television must always be derivative, because the media does not devote the time and study to original research which academics customarily do. As a writer, I usually find myself commentating for television or writing for newspapers about issues I have researched on my own account, and that goes for most of us who do this sort of thing. The majority of television programmes about history are researched, written, filmed and edited within a span of say, three or four months for one hundred minutes of air time. The gestation period before work starts and the lag before transmission will usually, of course, extend any given project to a wider time frame. Remarkably little of the labour involved is devoted to original research. That is almost invariably cribbed from a book written either by the presenter, or by somebody else. The most frustrating aspect of making television programmes, for a writer, is that vast energy is devoted to the technical process of translating his or her thoughts onto the screen, visualising what he or she wants to say, and very little to intellectual activity. In a good day of filming pieces to camera, with retakes and the usual technical difficulties, it may be possible to record say, 400 words' worth of script. The production process almost invariably involves honing down a mass of complex thoughts and ideas into a series of much simpler and briefer ones.

In the case of newspapers, it is unusual nowadays for there to be longer than a week between a title, even a broadsheet, commissioning a piece – even one of say three thousand words – and its appearance in print. Newspapers usually come bottom of the derivative food chain in their treatment of history. That is to say, if a television programme is constructed around the expertise of the author of a book, a newspaper piece is very frequently precipitated by the appearance of a television programme. Often, the producer of a programme will generate advance publicity by giving details of his wares to a single title. It is unusual, nowadays, for a newspaper specially to commission historical pieces, save to commemorate wartime anniversaries.

Maybe this is partly because the work of some professional historians for newspapers is unreliable. I remember once, as an editor, commissioning two big pieces for an anniversary from a celebrated historian for a fat fee. When his articles arrived, in despair I took two days off to sit at home rewriting them. I had then to pass the torch to an Assistant Editor, who spent another two days on them before they were finally fit to appear. A few weeks later, I happened to meet the author at a party. He said loftily: 'I think those pieces of mine came out rather well, don't you?' I stifled an expletive. He seemed to suppose that turning his gobbledegook into publishable prose was part of the service to be expected from us. I will not suggest that this episode reflected any universal truth about scholarly writing. But more scholars would gain greater access to the media, if they would take more trouble to render their work comprehensible to the lay audience. The only reason people like me are in steady work is that we possess some ability to convey information to the public in a way the public can understand, even though we are generally less informed on a given subject than many academics. We provide a bridge, however rickety, between scholarly research and a wider public.

Oddly enough, I don't think journalists are nearly as much resented by academics as are holders of tenure who themselves contribute to the media. A jealousy and resentment of telly dons by non-telly dons has informed the relationship since at the least the days of A.J.P. Taylor. Yet nothing could do more for the service of history and its teaching, than for more academics to develop the skills of presentation for television and newspapers, in such a way as to force out people like me as middlemen. The recognised scholarly historian will always possess an authority and credibility that most journalists cannot aspire to. If more academic historians could overcome an instinctive disdain for the media, and for the compromises that are inescapable in working with it, they would do great service to their own trade as well as to their bank balances.

Yet it would be naïve not to acknowledge an understanding of why many academics feel such distaste for the media. I was dining recently among a group of distinguished historians, and even in casual conversation in an Oxford senior common room, I felt strongly aware of their hostility to the press especially, admittedly intensified by recent events involving Cherie Blair. It is a cliché to describe journalism as a first rough draft of history. Journalism has always represented a balance between information and entertainment. In recent years, and to the dismay of many journalists, the balance has tilted more sharply towards entertainment at the expense of information, even in supposedly serious newspapers. I have always thought it wrong to blame only editors and proprietors and the bosses of television companies for this. Readers and viewers have a hand in it, too. They show an extraordinary eagerness to pay good money for trivia, and a diminishing enthusiasm for watching or reading heavyweight journalism, especially when it pertains to politics. Newspapers and television companies are not charitable concerns. They cannot be expected relentlessly to force down the throats of the paying public a diet it does not want.

*   *   *

The demands to leaven dry facts with entertainment, which has always been there, seems to grow more insistent with each generation. Most teachers of English literature testify to their pupils' expectations that they will be able to watch the video in tandem with reading the book. It is necessary to work with this reality, however much one may lament it; and of course, it is at least as true of history. All of which is but another way of saying that history and the media need each other, and that academics, journalists and programme-makers need to talk to each other about how we can best serve each other, and the public, above all by bringing the fruits of historical research to a popular audience. I have spent enough of my life among academics, to feel the worm of envy to which I referred at the outset. I shall never myself attain any pinnacles of scholarship. The years I have spent in newspapers and television have taught me a great deal about their limitations – but also a lot about their thrilling opportunities. If a new generation of professional historians can learn to exploit those opportunities, and if programme-makers and newspaper editors can give them the freedom to do so, there are wonderful mountains out there for all of us to seek to ascend.

# 8

# The Past on the Box: Strengths and Weaknesses

*Ian Kershaw*

History has never been more popular. Measured by the size of a mass audience open to at least brief and superficial exposure to history through its treatment on television, the assertion is probably true. In recent years the number of programmes on historical topics shown on television has grown enormously. The best of these are usually shown on mainstream, terrestrial television, and draw millions of viewers. Sold on to foreign TV companies, reproduced on video (official and home-made), repeated at intervals, used in schools and universities, a critically acclaimed television documentary can reach worldwide audiences of upwards of fifty million people. No history book, however acclaimed, however popular, will reach such an audience. But television is certainly a way to sell history books. A successful television series will generally spawn a successfully selling book. For the presenters, fame as well as for-tune beckons. So it is scarcely surprising that television holds out great attractions to those historians keen to exploit the potential of television for popularising their own areas of interest, knowledge and research.

It is also not surprising that eyebrows are raised or witheringly dis-missive remarks heard in the academy about the superficiality of the treatment of this or that aspect of the subject in question, about the pre-senter's ignorance of the latest research findings on some arcane mar-ginalia, or that the programme has failed to take into account quite different interpretations – notably, one's own. For, remarkable as it might seem, even academics can sometimes harbour petty jealousies and perhaps occasionally repress the secret wish that they might have been the chosen ones to present history on 'the box'. But the almost inevitable criticism by professional historians whenever television his-tory is discussed is not just a product of envy. It reflects a real tension between the professional discipline of history, in its central focus on research and teaching, and the popularisation of history through the mass media. It even touches on the very purpose of history, and whether – horror of horrors – television might in some way be serving that purpose better than academic history.

At first glance, history's current popularity also seems to embrace the academy. There are many more historians in post at British universities than was the case three or four decades ago. Far more books and scholarly articles on history are produced than used to be the case – many of them, of course, 'encouraged' by the dreaded Research Assessment Exercise. History at university is one of the more sought-after degrees. Good departments have no difficulty in attracting large numbers of well-qualified students (though the postgraduate scene is less rosy). Whether television plays any part in the appeal of university history is unclear. But it certainly does nothing to dampen history's attractiveness as an academic discipline. Beneath the surface, however, history as a professional discipline is less sure of itself. As the discipline has expanded, embracing new historical themes far from what used to be taken as the essence of the curriculum, and with a marked defensiveness prompted by the gnawing self-doubts created by post-modernist philosophies, it has become ever less clear and more open to dispute precisely what that discipline is, what a university history syllabus should comprise, and what purpose history serves. 'Professional history', in the estimation of David Cannadine

> is in danger of collapsing under the weight of its unwieldy erudition; more and more historians know more and more about less and less; most scholarly articles and monographs have a readership of twenty and a shelf life of five years; academic history, as taught and practised in universities, increasingly appears to outsiders to be at best incomprehensible, at worst ridiculous.[1]

These strictures on the narrowness and introversion of specialist history implicitly form part of a plea for the popularisation of the past. One of the early popularisers of history – for there was, of course, 'popular history' before television – was the Cambridge historian, G.M. Trevelyan (author of a best-selling book, among others, on the social history of England). For Trevelyan, historical research was not an end in itself. 'If historians neglect to educate the public', he stated, 'if they fail to interest it intelligently in the past, then all their historical learning is useless except insofar as it educates themselves'.[2] Another populariser, and early exponent of the up-and-coming medium of television, was the recently deceased Hugh

Trevor-Roper, who, in his Oxford inaugural lecture in 1957 was emphatic that the ultimate purpose of history is to educate and edify a non-professional audience.[3] And at the time, of course, no one was more adept at this than Trevor-Roper's arch-rival, A.J.P. Taylor, the first real 'telly-don'. His hallmark – the unscripted lecture without props or visual images – was idiosyncratic enough then, and would probably not work on television now. But the stars of a much more elaborate (and expensive) present-day television history, the Schamas, Starkeys and Fergusons, follow in Taylor's footsteps and have inherited the mantle of those who believed long ago that the historian's job was to use their skills and knowledge to bring big and important historical themes to the attention of a mass audience. Though the tension between popularisers and specialists has always been there – plenty of Lucky Jims pursued their arcane specialisms even while the Trevelyans and Taylors wrote for a mass readership among the lay public – it has been magnified by the present-day centrality of television in our lives, and the ways it can portray history.

Television is in many ways a marvellous medium to depict history. Certainly, it is an extraordinarily powerful medium. The plasticity and immediacy of the visual images make an impact more vivid than that of even the most majestic of prose passages. The careful, critical analysis of the historian cannot compete in gripping excitement with eye-witness interviews on dramatic events. Two instances come to mind from the series *The Nazis: A Warning from History*, on which I worked with the extraordinarily talented producer, Laurence Rees. In one unforgettable sequence, an elderly Lithuanian described before the cameras what it had felt like when, many years earlier, he had shot Jewish women and children on that very spot. In another, a woman was effectively forced to admit on camera, confronted with her own report, that she had denounced a neighbour to the tender mercies of the Gestapo – and for nothing more than that she invited some odd friends to her apartment, and looked Jewish. In each case, a few seconds of television coverage could convey a message more movingly and starkly than acres of print.

Through the virtual reality of computerised reconstructions we can now also be transported back into ancient temples and pyramids. We can be ferried round the world quite literally from one second to the next on television to follow history on precisely the sites where it was made. Television history, in short, contains an inbuilt drama that the lecture-room, seminar discussion, or research monograph are scarcely equipped to match.

\*    \*    \*

But television also has serious weaknesses from the perspective of a professional historian. While unquestionably powerful, it is of necessity superficial. Constraints of time alone determine this. Programmes have to be fast-moving if they are to retain their viewers – and the viewer figures are seen by TV bosses as practically the only criterion of the success or failure of a programme. The 'treatment' (or script) for a fifty-minute 'show' (as programmes, even on the most horrific or moving aspects of history, are called) is as a rule only twenty or thirty pages long – scarcely the length of a pamphlet, let alone a book. So there is little room for elaboration, differentiation or qualification. Vital aspects of explanation have to be summarised in a single line of text, to the backcloth, of course, of the pictures, for these are the key determinants of how the film is constructed. Outstanding archival footage will ensure that certain passages in the programme have relatively extensive coverage. By contrast, important elements of an explanation are often quickly passed over because of the absence or limitations of photographic material.

Beyond that, television is for the most part at its strongest where there is a dynamic narrative, a progressive story-line, and at its weakest where thematic or structural analysis is required, especially where an issue is highly contentious and subject to widely differing interpretation. The life-blood of a history seminar at university is disagreement and problems of interpretation. The tutor ideally guides the student towards an explanation through assessment of the strengths and weaknesses of argument. Television history is far more directive. Problems of interpretation tend to muddy the waters, and to leave the viewer confused, baffled, or at least unable to decide which of variant interpretations is the most valid. Disputatious talking-heads are generally seen to be an absolute turn-off. In a ratings-led medium, there is no room for this approach. Not least, television is generally interested in certain sorts of history which lend themselves to the dramatic, the spectacular, the macabre, the titillating, the intriguing, the stunning new discovery, the iconoclastic upturning of reputations. The focus usually falls upon the stories of individuals, and upon the description of important events. When these are allied to particularly striking footage and illuminating eye-witness accounts, the effect is invariably superb. Not for nothing do the two world wars – the defining episodes of the twentieth century – constitute history where television is at its best.

Even these, in television terms, are less sure of success than exploiting the undying interest in the pharaos and mystique of ancient Egypt. But although television has come to deal in far more interesting fashion with history before the twentieth century – before, that is, there was film footage – it is still most at home with very recent history. So large tracts of history are not easy for television to represent, and because popular interest is for the most part more geared to very modern history, television producers are less keen to make programmes on earlier eras – in fact, that is, on most of the course of history. Even in the modern era, television producers are unlikely to rush to tackle some themes – bureaucracy would be one obvious example – which are scarcely peripheral to historical understanding (and naturally have to be dealt with by professional historians), but have no pictorial value or obvious viewer interest.

So from a professional historian's point of view, television history has enormous strengths, but also significant weaknesses. Yet if historians agree that the purpose – or at least one major purpose – of history is to take the subject beyond specialists in the academy, then they must look with some favour upon the medium which, *par excellence*, is capable of doing just that. Historians are not dealing with mysterious or intractable matter (though sometimes they might give the appearance of doing so). They should want to communicate it in terms that non-specialists can understand (while, of course, not prostituting their material). With the exposure in the mass media and the bold statement rather than the cautious half-assertion on a highly specialised point, ring-fenced with qualifications, comes, it must be admitted, the danger of criticism which many historians are glad to avoid by publication of learned articles or monographs reviewed by their friends and colleagues. But some at least of the frustrations of historians with television can be avoided. An apparently flattering invitation to be interviewed by a TV company for a film in production does not have to be accepted without some careful research on the company, the film itself, the control over the input, and – most importantly – the experience and ability of the producer. This might avoid considerable expenditure of time for minimal (or no) remuneration before realising that one's contribution has been minimalised and distorted through being taken out of context, or that the programme has, in fact, not even been commissioned.

Historians involving themselves in more than a peripheral way in television documentaries – let alone feature films where the 'facts' can all too inconveniently get in the way of the story-line – need to ensure above all that they have an appropriate level of control over the final output. TV companies want academic legitimation for their history programmes. They are essentially exploitative – using historians' contributions where it suits, ignoring them where it doesn't. Historians generally have no say in how their contributions are used. But without care it is easy to provide backing for a programme which might damage rather than enhance a reputation. One of the pleasures for me in working on *The Nazis* was that Laurence Rees incorporated me from the outset not only in all aspects of planning and devising the programmes, but also in checking and criticising the film rushes, not just the scripts. In this way, it was a genuine partnership of a kind which, to my experience, seldom happens when historians work for television.

On the other hand, however, historians have to try harder than they often do to understand what television can and cannot achieve, and to work consciously to help to shape the programme in a medium which is not natural or familiar to them instead of expecting a fifty-minute programme to do the job of a five hundred-page book. Televisual history is different from 'print history' (though the rules of evidence are the same). But it has its own validity as a representation of the past. It would be as well if the professionals accepted this, saw the problems of condensing complex material and working to a visual imperative as a worthwhile intellectual challenge, and saw the creative tension in writing and production as highly stimulating. There is no need to feel exploited by television. Good producers will adapt to what can and cannot be done. Ultimately, these producers need professional historians, and their unsung, unspectacular, meticulous research and knowledge acquired through Socratic interchange with students, more than the historians need television. But nor is there any justification for being dismissive about television history. Some remarkable documentaries – *The World at War* is one – will stand the test of time which most history books will eventually fail. History on television is here to stay. If historians do not help to mould and influence it, others will.

## Notes

1. David Cannadine, *G.M. Trevelyan – A Life in History*, London, 1992, p. 184.
2. Cited in Cannadine, *Trevelyan*, p. 184.
3. H.R. Trevor-Roper, *History: Professional and Lay*, Oxford, 1957, esp. pp. 14–16.

# 9

# A Deep and Continuing Use of History

*John Tusa*

I have worked as a journalist and broadcaster. I have managed broadcasters and arts administrators. Yet I still think of myself as, deep down, a historian. I hope I am entitled to do so. I assume the term 'historian' is not the monopoly of those who make their living from writing, teaching or studying history. I assume there is no closed shop, no medieval craft guild of historians, no restrictive coterie of like-minded pedants and obsessives. I hope history is, rather, an activity open to all those who feel a clear affinity for it, a strong connection with it, a passing if distant connection with its skills and disciplines, without defining too closely what kind of history they particularly enjoy or how they use what remains of their historical skills. Rather like Hamlet's Player King, we can offer history that is comical, tragical, conceptual, economical/ pastoral, social/statistical, personal/psychological, political/polemical, epical/mystical, chronological/conventional, demographical/folklorical, and many combinations besides. (Spare us, though, from 'heritage' history, from 'Merrie England', from the 'Beefeater' or 'Vanity Fair' school of fantasising about the past.) There is, no doubt, room for all these in the great tent of history and only the mean-minded stand as intellectual thought police at the tent flaps and quiz the credentials of those who wish to enter.

For who is to judge who is a proper historian and who is not? Most of those who fill the reading room of the Public Records Office at Kew are searching for the origins of their family, often for traces of a particular family member, especially from world war regimental records. These lovers of their personal history may never produce anything of substance from their researches even in an obscure parish magazine or regimental newsletter. But to misquote Dr Johnson, 'few people are more innocently engaged than when studying family history'. I had a happy

124

moment myself in this respect only recently. I was preparing for an interview with Tom Stoppard. I knew that like me he was Czech by birth. I knew that our fathers had both worked for the Bata Shoe Company, in its home town of Zlin in southern Moravia in the 1930s. I think I knew that Stoppard Père – actually Eugen Straussler – was a company doctor. But it was only when I discovered that he worked at the company hospital, a cottage hospital in effect, and looked at the dates that he was there that I realised there was a fifty–fifty chance that Stoppard's father – Dr Straussler – had actually delivered me.

I have observed the joy of discovery too. On one occasion, my wife and I were in the reading room at Kew, shrouded as it is in the institutional, soporific calm of a hundred pencils passing softly over ruled paper or the soft susurration of feet shifting as readers wait for their files. Occasionally, there was the sound of the swifter scurrying of feet as readers tried to avoid David Irving. Suddenly, the ordered calm was broken. At a desk only a few feet away, a reader sat upright, and let out a loud and very audible shriek of delight. It was followed by another and another. No reading room supervisor hurried over to explain the rules of quiet working; no neighbour glared and shushed. Rather, several faces looked up, registered the event, and smiled a private smile of shared satisfaction. Something had been discovered. Perhaps something had been understood. I do not know what. It would have been intrusive to ask. It would not have mattered to me. But it mattered to him. I like to think the discovery was – on however small a scale – a moment of history. Had anyone asked me at Cambridge why I was reading history, I would not have replied that I expected it to be useful in later life. To the further question of why I was reading it at all, I might have replied that it was enjoyable, it was interesting and I seemed to have been surrounded by it since childhood.

\*   \*   \*

It was, naturally, history of a specially focused kind, as you get in all families which incline to a historical sense, or at least to a sense of their past. And particularly when your family changes countries, awareness of another place, another past, has a particular intensity to it. It was certainly presented with a grand historical sweep in our house. I come from a partly Protestant family from southern Moravia; my mother was convinced that her Hussite family had suffered from religious persecution for seven hundred years. My parents' adult years had all been in the fledgling Czechoslovak Republic. The most frequent refrain to the running commentary on history they provided was of 'three hundred years under the Austro-Hungarian yoke'. Their sense of the past was based on large dollops of historical grievance, intense but never rancid. But references to the Battle of the White Mountain when 'the flower of Czech nobility was cut down' in 1621 were frequent at Sunday lunch. Jan Amos Kominski (Comenius) was a regular 'guest'. All this induced in me, as perhaps it was intended to do, a sense of piquant loss, of distress at the subsequent denial of three centuries of lost Czech promise, sub-sumed in the myriad nationalisms of the Austro-Hungarian Empire. (Though, it was conceded, the Czechs had their place; they were the best pastry cooks in Vienna and the most diligent civil servants.)

Not that my father at least did not benefit from it. To his dying day he had perfect, 'hoch-Deutsch' – how could you equip youth for the world outside if they spoke only Czech in 1918? On one occasion, when the Hof Zug – the Imperial Train – stopped at my father's village, he was patted on the head by the Kaiser. These were hardly full consolations for belonging to someone else's empire. It was the creation of the Czechoslovak Republic that liberated my parents from what they always saw as this historic Habsburg oppression. They were proud of the achievements of their short-lived twenty-year Republic from 1919 to 1939. 'We were lucky', my mother would say, 'we had the best years'. They witnessed and were agonised by the undermining and destruction of the Republic through opportunistic British appeasement and the 1938 Munich Agreement between Adolf Hitler and the British prime minister, Neville Chamberlain. His was not a name to raise over Sunday lunch. Lord Runciman came second in the pecking order of contempt.

Compared with these grand cycles of lunch-table history, being taught the real thing at school came as an anti-climax. English history was – it seemed – a thing of fits and starts, of shreds and patches. As taught by a reverend gentleman who doubled up his teaching load with Divinity, English history consisted of King Alfred, the Norman Conquest, Magna Carta, the Black Death, the Hundred Years War, and seemed to peter out soon after the Divine Right of Kings. How, incidentally, did the Reverend Mr Royce teach us Divinity? Was it through the bare and random mile-stones of the nativity, the raising of Lazarus, the feast at Cana, the Last Supper, and a passing nod towards Pilate's washing of hands? All impor-tant, of course, but hardly providing a coherent or complete narrative of the Christian story. That was the trouble, too, with prep school history. What happened to the gaps? What occurred in between these moments of stirring action interspersed with occasional cataclysm? How did one close the gaps, an unvoiced question that was only partially answered as the years went by? My history is still, I fear, a large canvas with many holes in it.

There was enough to come from subsequent history teachers – especially at Cambridge – to convince me that history was interesting, narrative history often threw up juicy scandals, and that life without it would be considerably more puzzling than it was. Who in the Cambridge History Faculty of the late 1950s could not have been enter-tained by John Kenyon's acerbic commentaries on the Stuarts, Jack Plumb's scandal-ridden accounts of Walpole, or, in only a slightly dif-ferent field, Nikolaus Pevsner's descriptions of the building of Aya Sophia? Even so, this was entertainment, almost guiltily enjoyable; history still did not feel useful – nor was it suggested that it should be – despite exposure to the minds of the likes of Peter Laslett, John Elliott, Michel Vyvyan and Walter Ullmann.

*   *   *

It was only during the 1960s, as a current affairs producer in the General Overseas Service of the then BBC External Services that the sense of the possible utility of history dawned. These were the years of the East–West missile gap, the Cuba Crisis, the fall of Khrushchev – on election night in Britain in October 1964, of all times – of the Sino-Soviet split, of deep, anxious analysis of Soviet institutions – which defied understanding – and Soviet intentions – which usually defied belief. Some of the most acrimonious debates centred on the possibility – or for some, the impossibility – of a split in the International Marxist-Leninist monolith between China and the Soviet Union. Both states and parties shared the same ideology; both spouted it; seemed to act on its basis; both fiercely repressed, and often murdered, those who doubted or publicly ques-tioned that ideology. Most observers conceded that something might be a little tense between the two poles of Marxist-Leninist belief. But a split, it was officially held, could not be countenanced. Communists did not split. They were bound by ideology; perhaps as pragmatic democrats, we were constitutionally incapable of comprehending how much ideologies erred from the path of pure dogma when politics demanded it.

The only evidence that there might be a historic schism, a rupturing of the tectonic plates below the seemingly solid crust of ideological unity, came in the texts of official party and government communiqués, speeches and resolutions. One analyst, Victor Zorza of the *Guardian*, maintained that the two centres of communism had irrevocably split over ideology and doctrine. Against bitter journalistic and diplomatic opposition, he built up his case for a split from close analysis of public statements from Moscow and Peking. It was not yet apparent in their actions, he argued; but the political implications of the schism would be huge if understood and acted upon. Nothing could be drier, more apparently formulaic than such analysis; nothing could be more carefully controlled; nothing could be more like a legalistic medieval doctrine from, say, the Papacy. Ah, yes, there it was. I had been here or hereabouts in the Mill Lane Lectures of Dr Walter Ullmann, reader in medieval history at Trinity. Ullmann, too, had pored over the papal documents to show that the seeds of the Papal/Imperial conflicts, the shifts in doctrine, the staking-out of future political positions, would always show up in the carefully buried words of official texts if you looked hard enough.

Ullmann knew that words mattered to institutions, which existed on words, doctrine or ideology. They were potent weapons in the struggle for power. They validated the argument, determined the victor and ultimately justified the use of power as the victor wished to use it. Victor Zorza understood this as well; the approach of the two men was identical. His prescient diagnosis of the Sino-Soviet split was not based on speculation but on hard textual evidence. He was ultimately completely vindicated. But as radio current affairs producers charted and debated these arguments over the airwaves, my instinct to believe that Victor Zorza was right, that his evidence was compelling, was based entirely on my experience of being taught by Walter Ullmann at Cambridge, whose analysis of a previous seismic split several centuries previously had been vindicated by events and history. It is not surprising that English politicians, diplomats and historians found difficulty with Zorza's and Ullmann's somewhat Central European legalistic approach to ideas and events. This is not the way the English use language or think about it; they enjoy a usage which is light, elusive, allusive, diverting and ambiguous. Language is about play. The idea that it had fallen into the hands of people for whom it won and meant power, and delivered the power of life and death over others, was puzzling and rather shocking.

*    *    *

Over the years, the debate about the nature of the Soviet Union surfaced in acute form in its declining years under Mikhail Gorbachev. Mrs Thatcher might believe she could 'do business' with him; when they met in Reykjavik, Ronald Reagan was ready to sell the whole US nuclear shop to him. But Gorbachev was still a Marxist-Leninist, wasn't he? And why should we trust these communist Russkis, people whom the West's ideological Right insisted on calling 'Soviets'? By the early 1980s, when I was working on BBC2's 'Newsnight' this was one of the questions of the day. You might be able to do business with Gorbachev; but could you trust him? Fortunately, there were texts to examine in the run-up to the 1985 Communist Party Conference in Moscow which I covered for 'Newsnight'. So we went back to the words. We read Gorbachev's lips. Even before it started, it was a moment of history, the first Communist Party Congress with openly available facilities for journalists. Most of the key texts we examined in advance of the Party Congress were available in the transcripts of the daily Summary of World Broadcasts produced by the BBC Monitoring Service at Caversham.

What was noteworthy about Gorbachev's speeches, and what leaped out from the page, was that these were not products of the party machine, couched in orthodox ideological formulae. The speeches were frequently off the cuff – imagine Brezhnev talking off the cuff! Khrushchev, yes, but not Brezhnev – they were direct, immediate, often face to face with workers or farmers and filled with practical references to the country's problems. On one occasion, Gorbachev ridiculed the rigidities of the central planning system. It misdirected resources so badly that bakers baked bread to fulfil their quotas, but much of the bakers' output of loaves was used as animal fodder to meet the farmers' own quotas. What a vast waste of national resources, made inevitable by the rigid diktats of the central planning system. This was not a Soviet party voice we were reading, but something new, something different, both in tone and substance. The conclusion seemed rather clear. Here was no party ideologue; here was a practical politician trying to address real shortcomings in a concrete way. There was no dogma, no theory, just pragmatic common sense. This was clear before the Party Congress began. Thereafter, interpretation of the event itself became comparatively easy. When Gorbachev's keynote speech proved identical in manner and in tone to his speeches in previous months, it was a safe journalistic bet that the USSR had changed. It had, though the true Cold War doubters were only finally convinced by the attempted coup against Gorbachev in August 1991.

A very similar process was taking place in China in the early 1980s. The question posed – both political and journalistic – was identical in kind. How deep, how radical, how market-oriented was the policy of agrarian reform? Were farmers being freed from the chains of collectivisation and state control? Was it conceivable that the Party, which had introduced Collectivisation, the Great Leap Forward and the Cultural Revolution, would suddenly reverse its policy towards individual entrepreneurship – at least in the countryside – and allow it to flourish? Once again, the key documents, though still framed in fairly orthodox ideological terms, pointed strongly in one direction; namely, that the Communist Party leaders in Beijing had decided that the countryside could only flourish if farmers were given a free hand. But the Party would still keep a tight control on industry and the cities. It was liberalisation on two tracks, two-speed reform. Of course, I was not the only journalist who saw these trends. But I do know that clear memories of how Walter Ullmann pursued his esoteric analysis of medieval documents gave me real confidence in judging contemporary political documents and assessing policies from a very different time and place.

Nor am I alone in this experience. My son – also a product of Cambridge history – reminded me of an early research note he wrote for his city firm about the notorious Westland Helicopter affair that nearly split the Thatcher Government in the mid-1980s. Michael Heseltine dramatically walked out of the cabinet; Leon Brittan was moved on and sideways to the European Commission in Brussels. This was no small matter, a true Tory war between the 'great beasts' of the party. The only way to understand this intensely confusing issue, which was industrial, European and political all at once, was – my son believed – to establish what happened in exact detail. His sources were the newspapers; the method was chronological; the ensuing connection between individual actions, public statements and subsequent events provided a degree of clarity which no amount of interpretation or examination of investment business plans would ever have yielded. City company analysis is, in practice, heavily biased to engineering and financial analysis. In the light of his experience, the historical/political approach yielded explanations to the analysis of business/political decisions that were not available from other disciplines.

But the historical parallels go further. My son's special subject was 'Government, Industry and the Arms Race, 1860–1918'. As a City analyst in these areas today, he finds that every single shortcoming of contemporary arms procurement, every dispute over resource allocation for defence, every debate about investing in weapons in peace to insure against war – every issue is replayed in minute detail as it was one hundred and fifty years ago. All the same attitudes, the identical prejudices and, of course, the same mistakes are repeated despite the available lessons of history.

\* \* \*

This may well demonstrate the familiar cliche that journalism is the first rough sketch of history. I have no difficulty with that as a definition. It may also show something else – that history should underpin the first sketches of journalism, a very different proposition. But there are many journalists who are not historians, some of them fine journalists. I believe that being a historian will not by itself make you a good journalist; but I do conclude that the best journalists will have a historian's sense somewhere inside them. It may not be a precise historical sense, but it should involve at least a sense of time passing, of time involved in the perspective of events, of time as a partner in events, a shaper of actions. 'Haven't we seen all this before?' People are remarkably resistant towards admitting that the same mistakes can be made time and time again. If life is, as was once observed, 'one damn thing after another', then so is history, and the 'after' is crucial. Time is not a random agglomeration of moments; it is a connected and orderly sequence of moments, and human actions exist in that sequence and can often be best understood within it.

Yet, too much contemporary journalism and political management is oriented towards future events, rather than recording and reporting events that have happened. This trend was identified in Michael Frayn's Fleet Street novel *Towards the End of the Morning*, which caught exactly the moment when reporting changed from 'Yesterday, the Prime Minister said...' to 'Today, the Prime Minister will say ...' No one would say that *The Times* or any other broadsheet of our times is a 'Journal of Record'; they are, far more accurately, 'Journals of Today's Expected Engagements' , or desperate attempts at prediction not too far from Old Moore's Almanack. What is behind this attempt to reverse the flow of time, the narrative of events, to turn history back to front? This devotion to predictive journalism – 'We'll give you tomorrow's events today' – came a spectacular cropper on 9/11. Yet even after that apparently unexplainable and apparently unpredictable cataclysm, one that desperately needed understanding and explanation, the easier and often the more frequent response was to turn to forecasting and prediction. Could it happen again? Yes. Would it happen again? Impossible to answer. The truth is that the outlines of an answer are far more likely to lie in historical examination of the past rather than wholly unfounded speculation about the future. But as the great *Manchester Guardian* editor C.P. Scott didn't say 'Speculation is free but the past is expensive.'

Why do we seem to be reluctant to learn from the past, to prefer this unhistorical indulgence in speculation about the future? The most persistent indulgers in prospective presentation are Whitehall's spin doctors. They weave a perfect world in the future where targets once set are met, where promises made are delivered, where predictions become fact, where objectives turn into outcomes. In this view, the prediction of the future is preferable to the history of the past. By defiantly asserting what tomorrow will bring, the spinners are indulging in a childish fantasy based on word magic – if you use the words with enough belief, then the world will change to become what you say it will become. It also reflects a belief that by trying to conjure up a reality of things that will happen, this supersedes the brutal actuality of the past where the best laid plans, five year plans, key deliverable, predicted outcomes turn into dust and disappointment. The subsequent effort of managing such massive disillusionment caused by policy failure is too great; far better to stick to the hoped for fantasies of the perfect tomorrow. In this respect, today's Whitehall and Washington spinners are of the same self-deluding species as yesterday's communist central planners. To say that something will be so, will make it so. The plan has been decreed; the plan will be delivered. It is a kind if word magic. Both spinners and planners ultimately fail because they try to turn their backs on events as they turned out and on history as it happened.

If Harold Macmillan knew too much history, John Major knew too little. It was well said of the latter by a cabinet colleague: 'We have tried having a Prime Minister who knows nothing, and do you know, it doesn't work.' Tony Blair, by contrast, knows some history but it is very selective; it tends to focus on a history of past Labour defeats. That bit of history must not be allowed to repeat itself; so like out-of-date generals, he fights a defensive war to avoid a defeat that is inconceivable anyway. By concentrating on the experience of a single event, Blair misses the opportunity to learn more broadly on other fronts.

*    *    *

The connection between history and politics and journalism is – or should be – obvious enough. But the thought that history might be useful in management was less predictable. Before I became managing director of the BBC World Service in 1986, I had not reckoned that a sense of history could be a key tool in managing that institution. After all, this was an organisation that had its origins in a sense of connection with empire; it grew as a body engaged with the struggle with Fascism; it developed as an institution that faced communism in the Cold War. Beyond that it needed a philosophy that could encompass the political controversies of decolonisation, controversies with an acutely painful domestic political edge to them. It required a voice that could report the collapse of international communism but would not be a committed player in the process. Each of these great historical phases had dominated the editorial concerns of the BBC World Service for a decade or more. It would have been tempting to see the World Service as just a chameleon organisation, without an organising principle behind it, responding to outside events as they demanded. Yet this seemed to me both an inadequate way of defining it, and not a way that would survive for a long time. Opportunism has its value. It risks exposure as being without principle of a more enduring kind. And a truly great organisation deserves better than a reputation for fleet-footed opportunism.

I believed that there was a unifying principle behind the World Service's work, that it underlay all its historical phases, and that this principle needed drawing out and expressing if it was to survive into the future. But this principle had to be reintegrated into the World Service's history, its editorial practices, its own self-image, in order to create an understanding of what it had done, as well as create a justification for what it could continue to do. The organising principle was not hard to find – the provision of accurate information, as unbiased as possible, to meet the needs of an information-starved audience, without direct government interference. I could without difficulty knit the various phases of World Service evolution together around this unifying theme. I did not believe that I was distorting the experience of my predecessors. It was a head of the German Service during the war who insisted that the truth about Allied losses in the early years must be reported, because – as he put it – 'if we report our defeats, then they will have to believe us when we report our victories'.

There were, of course, those who saw no problem with broadcasting propaganda back to the Germans, who delighted in setting up clandestine transmitters which mimicked the characteristics of domestic Nazi stations, and fed back misleading news or actual disinformation. Muriel Spark has written about this memorably in her autobiography. It was clearly very enjoyable to do and it was by no means ineffective. Yet as a justification for broadcasting overseas, it did not have an enduring quality to it. It was too opportunistic, too limited in its applications. There were others who saw counter propaganda as both politically necessary and morally right at a time of mortal national peril. Equally, there were many during the Cold War who saw intellectual engagement with the adversary – proving that they were wrong intellectually – as essential and anything less as stupid and morally contemptible. My own view was that the real, moral principle behind BBC overseas broadcasting which defined it from others was that it offered listeners the opportunity to make up their own minds. Colleagues who shared this view during the Cold War insisted that you could hardly expect listeners to take you seriously if you were telling them, in effect, that they were fools to believe what their own broadcasters told them. That was for the listeners to decide on the basis of the accurate information the broadcasts offered.

By the late 1980s, the World Service needed a unifying principle to explain its work. There was a good deal of historical reminiscence and folklore lying around. There was nothing that attempted to pull it together into a single narrative, to use it to make the organisation work more effectively. We needed one story to explain what we were doing. Fragments of that story existed in World Service folklore, in canteen gossip, in BBC Club drinking sessions, in the intense local memories of the thirty-seven languages in which – other than English – the World Service then broadcast. From General De Gaulle broadcasting his appeal to resist to France in 1940; to the full reporting of national opposition to Eden's invasion of Suez in 1956; to Solzhenitsyn's criticism of Anatol Goldberg's commentaries on the Soviet Union for being too wishy-washy; to the communist infiltration of the BBC Portuguese Service; to Mark Tully's expulsion from India during the Emergency – these were the internal fables that resonated around the building. They needed organising into a coherent whole.

Management involves telling an organisation a story which it recognises as being a true account of itself; and then telling the outside world the same story. The consistency of the message is essential; and its use both inside and outside the organisation is essential too. You can't have one version in private and another in public. The validation is both internal and external, each reinforcing the other. Without that consistency, the organisation becomes, and is seen as being, dysfunctional and contradictory. I used the opportunity of lecturing invitations to talk through a series of World Services policy issues; they ranged from defining the difference between information and propaganda; facing the challenge from censorship and jamming of broadcasts; assessing the way that international broadcasting was used and abused; and looking at how our approach to international broadcasting had altered over the previous forty years. Though the lectures were not written in such a coherent order, they did act as essential pieces of intellectual ground clearing for the larger project of creating a universal message for the World Service. Articles justifying our broadcasting to Latin America, or to Western Europe had a more detailed focus, a more tactical purpose. Gathering the material for these essays involved tapping into the knowledge and experience of those who worked at Bush House, drawing out what was on occasion almost oral history, knowing that it was being saved from extinction, and engaging staff in the articulation of an account of what they did. This was not a historical account imposed from above but one sought from below.

The historical understanding that we all gained from this process of recovering and articulating our history had three purposes. First, it helped Bush House to explain to itself why it was there, what it was doing, and why it could continue to lay claim to public funding. Today, you would call it the Vision and Mission Statement. Second, armed with this understanding, it could argue more effectively with the Foreign and Commonwealth Office, not only that operational editorial independence was part of the fabric of the institution but that it was the only guarantee of its utility and effectiveness. Finally, it answered all the questions from friends and critics alike about whether we were truly editorially independent. Yet even such a thorough process was not enough. As the 1980s went by, an even more pressing question emerged. Did the BBC World Service have a role at all once the Cold War was over and communism had collapsed? By reviewing our history and defining our role in relation to it, we had a broad view of our purpose or function and our relationship with listeners anywhere. Put simply, it was free and reliable information in an information-starved world. Such a definition was not limited by a particular historical event, and was certainly not defined by political considerations such as 'winning the Cold War' or anything like it.

As a result of this process, by the end of the 1980s, the BBC World Service was positioned very clearly in a way that was consistent with its past, and rooted in its own historic record. Those rival broadcasters which defined themselves primarily in terms of winning the ideological conflict all fell by the wayside. It was not just that Radio Beijing and Radio Moscow lost their audiences after communism fell – they had always been simply incredible – but so did those once powerful arms of US external propaganda, Radio Liberty and Radio Free Europe. RL broadcast to the Soviet Union; RFE to the rest of the socialist bloc. Both were defined as 'surrogate radios', giving the listeners in socialist countries an alternative to their own domestic services. Both were very popular; both were effective in their own way. This propaganda way of broadcasting was in line with American beliefs. But it died as the Cold War died. The defining philosophy was too narrow and contradictory. Once the nations in question had their own radios, the surrogate broadcasters had defined themselves out of existence. Besides, once the conflict had been 'won' – if winning was the essence of the activity – then the broadcasting died as a parasite does when the host is killed. The fact that the World Service survived the collapse of communism and continues to flourish in an information-rich world was made possible by the repositioning of the Service in the late 1980s. It was a process based on a historical understanding of the kind of organisation it was, and deducing from its past those characteristics which would breed strength in the future.

There was a further historical process that could take place only after the fall of the Berlin Wall in 1989. During the years of ideological control, it was almost impossible to conduct research into the impact of international broadcasts on closed societies. We could guess how they had worked but we could not be sure. With the Wall down we could talk to those who had relied on the 'Voices', as they collectively called the foreign broadcasters, and piece together what the exact nature of the experience, political, personal and psychological, had been. We collected this history while it was still fresh in people's minds. While there were some surprises in what our listeners said, their experiences provided a solid confirmation about the nature and the scale of the impact of free information on open minds in closed societies.

*   *   *

If I had any doubt about the usefulness of history to management, it was provided by the John Birt years at the BBC. These were the days of 'Year Zero', an apt phrase, referring as it did to the Pol Pot destruction in Cambodia, a process aimed at eliminating a sense of history from the organisation. These were the years when anyone with a distinguished record within the BBC – part of the collective memory, part of accumulated experience – someone such as the former controller, BBC Radio Three and director of the Proms, Sir John Drummond – was publicly disparaged by the Birtites as being 'tainted by experience'. Others, such as Sir Mark Tully, were dismissed as 'old soldiers polishing their medals'. In this managerialist view, in the best Henry Ford tradition, history was bunk, the past was an obstacle not a pillar, and anything worth doing could be written out on a clean sheet of paper, unpolluted by sentences and grammar but embellished by bullet points. This was management by assertion, not argument. The excesses, and the subsequent wholesale rejection, of the policies of the Birt years in the BBC – policies largely unchallenged at the time – are well documented. The fact that they failed because they had no sense of history, indeed were designed to remove and reject all institutional sense of history, is less often noted. But of the many reasons for their failure, another tended to be under-emphasised.

The BBC is a values-driven organisation with a profound sense of its own history. Birt was trying to force people to reject their own past and worse still to forget it. Their instinctive refusal to do either of those things led to a fundamental clash between what the BBC and its staff were and what they were being asked to do and to say they were. The deeply held values, rooted in two generations of public service, were internalised, not eradicated, and ultimately defeated the externally imposed, unhistorical, Birtite systems. Yet there were losses, and many human casualties in the a-historical process of managerial revolution. The next BBC leadership, under Greg Dyke, set up training courses to instil BBC values, based on an understanding of the past, for the benefit of those staff newcomers who had no one to turn to for that understanding.

On the whole, management as a discipline – which I doubt that it is – is weakest when it tries to do without a sense of history. It is a set of tricks that go out of fashion very rapidly because though they delight once, they are seen through the second time. But those who profess to teach management have, typically, little sense of or interest in history. Perhaps this is why management studies are more like examination of snake-oil remedies than serious intellectual theory. A historical study of them would undoubtedly reveal how thin, voguish and superficial they were.

\* \* \*

Undoubtedly, management consultants would have told me how to put right the very sick organisation that I found when I went to be managing director of the Barbican Centre in 1995. Their prescriptions would have been the usual mixture of vision, mission statement, strategic direction, corporate branding, internal communication and so on. Most of such processes are sensible enough but fail when they are applied by rote and without imagination or discrimination. These are the consultancy activities which gave us such insights as painting all BA aircraft tail fins in patterns belonging to every nation under the sun, except the United Kingdom; changing the Royal Mail's name to Consignia and then returning to Royal Mail; and altering the name of one of Britain's biggest accountancy and consulting firms to 'Monday' because, according top highly paid brand experts, 'Monday' is about 'coffee, croissants and innovation' rather than a hole in the head. I suspect that each of these ghastly, comic, and finally expensive errors could be shown, on deeper examination, to reflect a profoundly unhistorical way of looking at the activity and the organisation in hand. But that is another story for another occasion.

The Barbican's needs were to rise above the immediate crisis where a chief executive had been ignominiously sacked after reducing the staff to an abjectly low level of morale. The short-term crisis was acute but it could be overcome only by reconnecting the Barbican's staff to their own immediate history. This was not a lengthy history, less than fifteen years, but it still mattered. Staff needed reminding of why the Centre had been built; what the original ideals were, how these ideals had developed and how they could develop more strongly. Even where major changes of programming were taking place – as when the Royal Shakespeare Company decided to vacate the theatre for six months a year in 1995 – we explained our response in terms of the centre's own artistic evolution. We changed from a receiving house – where you hire out your facilities to anyone with the money – to a promoting house – where you engage the artistes and companies to form a coherent artistic presentation, and shoulder the box office risk in the process. We moved from a passive to an active role. Rooting the understanding of change in time in this way gave it a validity and a comprehensibility that made internal acceptance and external presentation easier.

The process at the Barbican has been significantly different from that at Bush House. There, the sense of owned history was deep, extensive and immanent. It needed articulation, expression and an acknowledgement that it was a vital part of the organisation's body and soul. At the Barbican, a place with a much shorter history, it was more a question of retrofitting the history to the place. I had to identify the sometimes opaque strands of continuity in the previous fifteen years, and persuade staff that they existed in a body with a creative history to it, rather than a series of public crises and disasters. Did I make anything up in the process? I don't think so. For here too, the story had to be recognised by those whose story it was. And the external audience was even more critical. They knew – because the journalists had written of them – that the Barbican was a basket case of crises. They had to be persuaded that my new presentation of the Barbican's story was not just a PR confection, a crude piece of artspin. It had to square with what they saw we were doing artistically; they had to be persuaded that this new account contained a deeper truth, a fresher and more important one, than the crises that had once obsessed and delighted journalists.

\* \* \*

I cannot write about my use of history without referring to those times when I have used it in a professional way while working with my wife on books about the Nuremberg Trial and the Berlin Airlift. We had many good moments, sharply historical ones. During the former, many people asserted, without evidence, that the United States had tried to take over the entire trial from its four-power organisation and run it themselves. There was no evidence that we knew, that confirmed this charge. As we interviewed a member of the US prosecution team, he went to his attic to get out some 'old papers'. He handed them over. When we read them, there was a document setting out in detail the proposed tactics for achieving that very US control of the proceedings that had been alleged but not previously established. We were mystified when William Hayter – former British ambassador to Moscow and much else besides – denied all involvement in intelligence activity in Berlin in 1948. The joy in discovering intelligence assessment papers at the Public Record Office in Kew with Hayter's name all over them was acute.

Enlightenment also came in unexpected ways. Who better to talk to about President Truman during the Berlin Blockade than his secretary of defence, Clark Clifford. When we met him in Washington, this rather grand Southern gentleman, a magnificent eighty-four years old, kept offices in the resonant firm of Clifford and Warnke, redolent of the Washington political establishment and clubland, with leather chairs, parchment lampshades, and drawn curtains. In the United States, old statesmen never die, they just withdraw to their law firm. Clifford put his fingers together, leaned back and drawing on the deepest recesses of his memory, gave us the vaguest and broadest recollection of 'some trouble with the Soviets'. Our hearts sank. Yet as the seer continued, we were transported back over the years to what the atmosphere of the time was, the mind set, the world view. The encounter did not provide a word for the book; but it did create some understanding which coloured what we wrote. Nothing could have been more different than the encounter with another bristling octogenarian, Paul Nitze. His famous 'walk in the woods' with his Soviet counterpart, Anatoly Dobrynin, opened the way for the SALT treaty limiting nuclear weapons. We found him after a long walk down a seemingly endless State Department corridor at Foggy Bottom. There he sat, warily, waiting for us. His opening words, 'Whaddya want to know'? were a challenge not an invitation. Mining oral history is not always easy even when you face a rich lode of information.

These more direct experiences of the use of history have been an important part of my life too, hugely enriching and entertaining. One part of me yearns to return to the soft scurrying of pencils at Kew, the weary but satisfied homeward plod on the eccentric North London line, the nostalgic smell of FCO documents, the frisson as you look at Ernie Bevin's scrawled note on a minute. This is the stuff of history as it was written, as it was created, as it waits to be rediscovered. But assuming that remains a dream, then the sheer fun, the understanding, the wisdom that a sense of history has given me in my working life is incalculable. I have found it a deep and continuing use of history. It would all have been far harder without it.

# 10
# Writing the History of Broadcasting*

*Jean Seaton*

When Jack Ruby murdered Lee Harvey Oswald, live, on television in November 1963, millions of Americans were turned into eye-witnesses of a momentous assassination – as if they had been there in person. Television 'broke down' barriers of distance and space – and showed audiences history being made in a particularly vivid way.[1] It took the audience to history. However, the dramatic tragedy also altered the status of audiences, involving them in an event in a way which seemed simple but whose implications were more complex than they appeared. In fact, the effects of this electronic intimacy have been irreversible and more widespread than is often recognised. Nevertheless, back in 1963 history was what TV showed. It was still possible, at that point, to see television as a transparent window on the world which merely displayed history happening somewhere else.

All sorts of barriers went down, once television started to roam. In an odd way, television has turned us all into slum-dwellers, living cheek by jowl with each other. We now expect to read the shadow which crosses the face of a president when told of a catastrophe. We expect to see leaders caught unaware: thus a prime minister's sweat-stained shirt may be found more eloquent than his carefully chosen words. As a consequence politicians rehearse their informal performances and we are hungry for what lies behind them – and complain about 'spin'. Over the twentieth century broadcasting remade the democratic political party – thus one explanation of the demise of local party structures is simply that leaders no longer need them – they appeal over the head of parties directly to audience-voters. At the same time democratic politics has shifted out of halls and assemblies into broadcasting-made spaces. College Green outside the Palace of Westminster and the Millbank television studios are new media-made debating theatres that carry more conviction and authority than the chambers of the Houses of Parliament. In a similar way we all applaud the demise of deference – but it has not collapsed because we are better democrats and one cause is that broadcasting tramples down barriers. But there have been other less obvious results too – after all it is very difficult to protect a child from adult behaviour in a television-watching society. The walls between children and adults are not sustainable when access to a screen reveals all that used to be shrouded in grown-up mystery. One may bewail the loss of innocence or applaud the realism, but both views are irrelevant – because unintentionally broadcasting has re-engineered social life.

Let us take a lighter example – the election evening broadcast of 1997, as Labour victories rolled in and Conservative safe seats fell. Viewers watched happy new Blair-babes but they also saw Conservative ministers watching television pictures of colleagues losing their seats. Audiences, via television, closely observed contenders for the leadership of the Conservative Party watching screens that showed them rivals being eliminated. Audiences could observe other players calculating what these events meant for their own careers. It was enthralling viewing, as real political drama unfolded, and many of the actors experienced exultant success or a kind of ruin, often with infectious amazement or stoic nobility and occasionally with a sickening vindictiveness. It was pure Athenian democracy. You could see the breathing and the quiver as men and women came to terms with their fate. Yet this thrilling election spectacle was virtual; it only happened via television and it only happened in a space that was electronic and between studios.[2] It was a skilfully crafted masterpiece of broadcasting. It was the people making the television choices, out of a deep understanding of the political realities and personalities, informed professional public service broadcasters who wove the event together out of men and women in town halls all over the nation. In this election moment broadcasting had become the theatre whose conventions (cutting from shot to shot, Michael Portillo mastering himself, Steven Twig's buttoned-up jacket scarcely containing the excitement) were what the politicians were performing politics within.

Finally, think of September 11. You will, of course, recall where you were when you first heard of the event, and how you then came to see it. It produced images of huge emotional and political impact. Although we can never know finally, it seems likely that the timing of the two planes that crashed into the World Trade Centre was calculated with publicity in mind, the first plane designed to attract attention and the second a little later to make sure that the cameras had had time to be assembled to record the disaster. Those that hi-jacked the planes were as concerned with the conventions of the news and as familiar with its habits as audiences. Like Christian martyrs in the arena they were using the universally understood habits of the dominant show for quite different purposes from those for which they had been intended. Part at least of the power of the event was that it was shown in real time – the real-life tragedy breaking before a bewildered audience as it happened. That Americans witnessed the attack – and experienced the alarming uncertainty as other attacks took place or seemed threatened – remade American politics; we still do not know for how long a period.

At first, on the morning of 9/11, broadcasters, as appalled and confused as anyone, had trouble in finding pictures or indeed making sense of what was happening. One veteran broadcaster in the BBC said that he simply could not find words to describe what was going on: 'I was tongue-tied, I simply could not get a word out at first. It was overwhelming.'[3] Yet when he did speak he represented professional, authoritative reason bringing a kind of order to chaos. By the time of the 10 p.m. evening news the BBC team had put together an account of the day that was accurate, comprehensive and told a complicated story with a deceptively simple elegance. Their explanation of the likely consequences of what had happened were so reliably composed that although they were framed within hours of the event they are still being worked out today.

\* \* \*

Thus there is a history of broadcasting as broadcasting. Broadcasting as a distinct and pervasive, cultural form, that frames much in contemporary life. The unexamined habits and practices of broadcasters do not simply provide a vehicle for showing us what is happening – they have now become central to political calculation (and many other aspects of our collective and individual lives) and the opportunities provided by the technology of broadcasting remakes institutions. That is, you cannot bolt the media on as an optional extra to 'proper' history – you can no longer do proper history without them, because they change everything. Indeed, at times broadcasting makes history rather than merely reporting it. Consequently one of the purposes of the history *of* broadcasting is to examine the ways in which broadcasting conventions, markets, innovations, choices, values and perceptions of audiences themselves mutate – because these things alter opportunities, and they influence what happens. Indeed, one aspect is to try and place the broad, long sweeps of media innovation in context beside the events that the media reflect and discuss – we need to know the history of broadcasting as a way of doing things, and the time-span of these changes may be quite long – even though the detail often evolves during the urgency of dealing with a particular crisis.

Thus live broadcasting, in real time from the scenes of the event, is now a ubiquitous format but one to which politicians, pop stars and sports have all had to adapt. Making things look as if they are 'just happening' is not easy, and as Paddy Scannell has perceptively pointed out, broadcasters have had to invent the ways of doing it.[4] The fact that we all take their conventions completely for granted is a testimony to how successfully they have managed it. The speeding-up of the news cycle is partly driven by technology and in one sense has just been progressing ever since the world was cabled in the 1860s. But in the last ten to fifteen years there has been an increase in this kind of coverage – because satellites can take pictures from distant places so quickly. We expect 'live' coverage of great news events – and often fail to recognise the significance of those not covered. Who was really moved by the fate of democrats under Saddam Hussein? We had no pictures of the cruelty and it went unheeded. Live coverage certainly has journalistic and indeed political consequences, and they are not all benign. Important news dies as quickly as trivial news; a faster cycle has meant that rumours float into the news more easily as journalists have less time to check facts, and so on.

Broadcasting history shows that communicating 'liveness' had to be constructed. This is partly organisational – how you co-ordinate cameras, pictures, sound and scripts. But it is also partly an intellectual discovery and a thought-through set of gestures that audiences recognise. It has origins in outside broadcasts that go back to the 1930s, to attempts to make sound broadcasting evoke the world of sport or ceremonial, and in games – but it also involves conceptions of audiences and their relationships to broadcasting as well. These developments and their consequences are the stuff of one key aspect of broadcasting history. The evolution of the ideas was brought about by broadcasters making decisions about practical, concrete issues – how to broadcast a particular event – yet the sum of such incremental innovations is larger than the parts. When the current events director of the outside broadcast of Princess Diana's funeral decided to break the previously agreed running order (thereby provoking a huge, nearly-broadcast, row) – and, on a hunch – panned out to the crowd outside Westminster Abbey applauding Earl Spencer, he made better television but he also made better political and public sense as well.[5]

Another rather different example, of a long-term trend whose origins can be traced in broadcasting, is what amounted to the industrialisation of celebrity production – and the 'production for destruction' personality cycle. There have long been media stars, but the market in fame has clearly evolved over the last twenty years – and television has been central to it. Those that TV builds up: the press tears down. TV constructs celebrity, but it has also become important to something less ephemeral and more valuable – achievement and reputation. There are very few successful careers now that do not have at least a minor media aspect. Yet the popular press fills its pages by destroying reputation. Moreover destroying reputation feeds off previous achievements and in a way just extracts further useful publicity value (for the media – filling pages and then screens quite as effectively as adulation) from the victim. Aspects of this modern media mobbing can be located in the precise moments when broadcasting itself started to deliberately feed the beasts – in America in the 1970s and in Britain in the 1980s. What changed was the sudden realisation by broadcasting and television press departments that the private miseries of humble soap stars, for example, were valuable publicity commodities. Once out of the bottle the genie of displaying private life for publicity advantage became irresistible and difficult to manage. Richard Sennett puts the origins of the psychologising of public life in the nineteenth century,[6] but we can also look at the role of soap operas like *EastEnders* and celebrity talk shows as antecedents of a contemporary theatre of cruelty. Broadcasting reveals (and composes) character – and has played an important part in elevating character estimation to a social pre-eminence.

An interest in oral history rose with radio and a concern with the uses of images rose with television. The media seep into our ways of thinking. Yet very often media stories or images are used unreflectingly, as if they were neutral evidence and an unproblematic clip of reality. They are frequently used to adorn or illustrate a narrative constructed somewhere else. Much as bits of old broadcasting are often used, of course, on many television programmes. This is not necessarily a problem, and audiences and history would not be well-served by a profusion of earnest little caveats about where pictures came from and how they were shot, or the development of the interview as a broadcast technique in the 1960s[7] (although these are all interesting in themselves). Yet the authenticity of what the audience is shown is an important issue in maintaining trust in the medium, and in Britain trust in broadcasting is very high. As Asa Briggs wrote, the history of broadcasting ought to have 'neither society nor broadcasting as background or foreground and not be done with hindsight'.[8] So the history of broadcasting should alert us all to the ways in which broadcasting standards change – because they influence how we perceive reality.

However, as well as the history of these – what we might call aspects of 'broadcastingness' – there is also the more conventional history of broadcasting as a puzzling, dominant, creative part of modern life. A set of institutions and a set of contents that help form contemporary experience. Broadcasting is so bound up with our pleasures and our duties that its reach influences (and is influenced by) every aspect of contemporary living. The British broadcasting industry is the second largest in the world; it is one of our leading export industries and one in which we are recognised to have real distinction. British television has been worth more to the economy than steel for nearly two decades – and of course plays an immeasurable role in promoting our values (and as propaganda for other goods and services that we produce). Meanwhile, British citizens consume on average forty-five hours of radio and television a week.[9] We spend more of our money on it than other societies.

Broadcasting has reflected our preoccupations and anxieties in soap-operas and drama, formed musical tastes, established new musical repertoires, set the standards for musical performance, told us how to raise our children, how to cook and what to laugh at. It has made us interested in archaeology and fans of snooker. It has been a vital part of our democracy, restlessly turning over social issues in many different formats. As Asa Briggs observed, 'To try to write the history of broadcasting in the 20th century is in a sense to write the history of everything else.'[10]

\* \* \*

Broadcasting has been made in institutions and these have always been shaped by governments and markets. Accordingly, the next level of broadcasting history has to concern the ways in which these institutions related to the outside world – both the market place for entertainment and the political world that sets the parameters of the industry. In Britain the history of broadcasting is also flavoured by the unique role it has been allocated in our constitution. Public service broadcasting – devoted to informing, educating and entertaining the public, dedicated to the pursuit of impartial and objective reporting, has been a central part of British social and political life for over seventy-five years. It has ensured that much of what we see and listen to is of a demonstrably higher quality than that in most other countries. It has often elicited and reflected on our preoccupations with a creative integrity. Perpetually involved in political wrangles of varying degrees of seriousness, it has nevertheless balanced an increasingly shrill press, and provided a kind of gold-standard of quality journalism against which other sources can be judged. At times, it has stood as a symbol of Britishness, so that the BBC's generally defendable compromises during the Second World War came to be seen as one of the achievements of the conflict, while the BBC's World Service is still recognised as an impartial authority all over the globe. (Thus since 9/11 the World Service audience has gone up by ten-fold in America and has doubled in the Middle East.)

None of this success has been accidental. For another, rather different, aspect of broadcasting history is not what the broadcasters have done but how they have been propelled, cajoled, encouraged and allowed to put making good programmes as a priority. For many years commercial broadcasters were obliged through regulation to meet very similar standards of public service to the BBC – so that they competed to make programmes, not just to make profits. Although much of this benign structure is being eroded, the sense that broadcasting ought to be fun and reliable, entertaining and truthful, provoking and steady remains, despite a good deal of political and commercial vandalism. Nevertheless, if you think of the British Rail system you can see that regulation often fails to deliver services – and explaining how and why successive governments and regulators have, on the whole, made some of the right decisions in British broadcasting is an important story. The decisions have been right because they have provided British viewers with better programmes that they have enjoyed more. Because of public service constraints and opportunities broadcasting addresses us as citizens, not just as consumers. In the past increasing competition has been managed with ingenuity, aligning new sources of revenue with new audiences and new kinds of programming at each new stage. Whether this continues to be the case is always an anxiety. It is a fragile and unique system that must adapt to a competitive world.

Of course sometimes things have gone wrong – and the consequences can be dire. Take ITN, the commercial company which invented British televised news as a popular and responsible form, and which for many years led the innovation in public service news provision (carefully isolated from aspects of damaging commercial pressure). It has recently been ruined by careless and economically blind decisions by short-sighted companies and regulators without the right powers. In this way a valuable source of impartial public information ingeniously created to attract audiences has been badly damaged. Even more perversely, greedy commercial companies have squandered a world-recognised brand – and consequently lost money. History is very useful here, for understanding how the key strategic issues that regulation and governments got right (or miscalculated) are a help in sorting out how policy ought to develop. Indeed, proper broadcasting history must attend to this policy climate: it is often indirectly quite as important in producing programmes as choosing writers or picking up trends; it sets the conditions for creative competition to flourish – or fail.

Broadcasting history is also concerned with the relationship of broadcasting institutions with successive governments – of different complexions. It is not a clear or straightforward relationship. One striking feature of writing and thinking about broadcasting is that very few foreigners remotely understand how it is that British public service broadcasting actually works – it is too implausible. How can the BBC maintain political independence when it relates to government? Yet it has. How do governments keep their hands off broadcasting when they have opportunities to interfere? Yet, on balance they have – or if they have done their worst, it so far has not been fatal to the BBC. The system has been fallible, sometimes the deal has been compromised, and there is always the danger that key decisions will destroy the essence of independence. Policy watchers tend to be Cassandras, always suspecting the worst. But the system has been so fruitful yet so finely balanced that it is not surprising that at any point many are gloomy about the prospects for survival.

Moreover, there are many press and broadcasting interests which always feel that things would be better for their businesses with a smaller BBC, less regulation, or no public service obligations. They have increasingly used the press to attack broadcasting. Tracing the history of press hostility is another aspect of writing the history now, one that was not as serious a threat in Briggs' periods as later. Between 2000 and 2002 the *Daily Mail* (whose readers watch more BBC programmes than those of any other daily newspaper), carried more articles attacking the BBC than any other paper.[11] What is going on? In the 1980s the *Sun* and *The Times* were unrelenting in their attacks on the Corporation, but the agenda was clearer then. But the steady drip of press hostility influenced tactics as well as the mood within the BBC.

The BBC has probably been protected by its success with audiences as a provider of fun that they appreciate and information they trust. Bill Cotton, the head of Light Entertainment at the BBC during the 1980s observed 'the best political protection is not a constitution but people out there switching on to programmes they like. Governments can't argue with that.' Thus broadcasting in Britain has survived in the middle of several constituencies: audiences, and politicians and its independent right to define the public good. But the BBC Governors are another reason the Corporation has succeeded. Although they have often been packed with sympathisers by political parties, and although from Reith onwards BBC management has frequently found them a nuisance, and although they have not always made the right decisions, nevertheless they have usually come to make good judgements that have defended the independence of the Corporation. Being on the inside they have a unique perspective, and usually just as they are about to go native on the Corporation there is some political row that has refreshed the perspective they bring to looking at affairs. They have been men and women who have made decisions that have, on balance, worked better than other more simple mechanisms: their human judgement has been fallible – but better than the alternatives. Yet looking at the history of the BBC one key relationship stands out: the quality of the Director General and the Chairman of the Governors and the quality of their relationship.

Then, while politicians come and go broadcasters, and broadcasting institutions – and so far the BBC – outlast any single government. But such a system is most compromised when oppositions are weak, and one-party rule extends over successive elections. Since 1979 this seems to have become the new shape of British democracy and it strains impartial institutions. Public service broadcasters have genuine problems when they have to go out and elicit opposition, or when they become the opposition – rather than being able to depend on one. (Many believe that the Civil Service is now under a real threat of politicisation and the issues are similar.)

From this perspective, broadcasting history can be seen as a sequence of political rows and threats – usually over single programmes, occasionally over tone and style, sometimes because of a long-running intransigent political problem – like Northern Ireland. The threats have often been all too real. A brief list of broadcaster versus government spats leads to some uncomfortable conclusions. For on every occasion of conflict – from the alleged left bias of the BBC in 1951, through to Suez, a raft of disputes with the Wilson government, the long slow poison in Ulster with the battles over programmes such as *A Question of Ulster, Real Lives* and *Death on the Rock*, conflicts over the reporting of the Falklands war, badly judged politically conventional programmes like *Yesterday's Men* – governments with majorities in the House of Commons have wanted to have the last word. And there have invariably been penalties (cuts in World Service budgets, the introduction of competition, reductions in the licence fee, the abolition of the IBA, the sacking of Director Generals, the replacement of Chairmen of the Board of Governors). It would therefore be naïve to think, as the BBC has seemed at times to recently, that being on the whole right in a bitter dispute is sufficient defence of the Corporation. But broadcasting has evolved through a kind of case law, and this has made it politically flexible. So threats have always been genuine, and may even now well prove lethal. Yet, although over seventy years governments have often had revenge, and done damage – nevertheless the system as a whole has survived because governments have also ultimately recognised its unique democratic value – and because, actually, sometimes something was awry in broadcasting.

*   *   *

The BBC is central to this broadcasting ecology and to writing its history. Partly this is because the Corporation has been a large and self-conscious organisation; partly because those that have worked for it have been so articulate (and writers of wonderful memos) and have found it part of their job to worry about why they are doing what they are doing. The BBC worries systematically about issues that are the very basis of democratic politics. But largely the BBC is central to writing broadcasting history because there is an archive that you can use – indeed a gorgeous set of archives – that illuminate contemporary history more vividly than any other. Most of the archive of commercial broadcasting has been dispersed along with the companies that used to make the programmes. Only at the BBC can you move within one file from *Muffin the Mule* to the prime minister, seamlessly. Or come across a great thinker's work being demoticised and given new weight by that careful elucidation and understanding of the audience that characterises all good broadcasting. Thus the work of the humane and influential child psychologist, Donald Winnicot, was translated into a new popular form by the producers of *Woman's Hour* at the end of the Second World War – they took his ideas, applied them to a crisis as men returned to the home after the war, and altered views of children and mothers for a generation. Broadcasting is expensive, collaborative, big-scale and gets made in institutions. Sometimes therefore it is the history of these organisations that also has to be looked at. So the next level is the organisational life within the institutions.

When Asa Briggs began his first volume of the history of the BBC published in 1961 there was little history of broadcasting anywhere available as a model – although a new interest in the media was stirring. Marshall MacLuhan was to publish *The Gutenberg Galaxy* in 1962, and Raymond Williams wrote *Communications* soon afterwards. Indeed, in a more important way there was little serious work on broadcasting at all, of any kind whether economic, historical, literary, sociological or political. There were memoirs – then, as now mostly written by rebels and refugees from broadcasting – invaluable sources, but partial. Briggs' work by contrast was the foundation of much more than the history of broadcasting – it was one of the bases of nearly everything subsequently written that treats the media seriously.

Briggs had already been a remarkably innovative historian, with little time for conventional disciplinary boundaries. He had written about culture and technology, people and cities and a whole sweep of social history. He also began the history of the BBC against the background of a post-war dispute about the legitimacy of 'official' histories of the war, which were, A.J.P. Taylor argued, compromised by the 'dead hand of the official agreement to vindicate not explore'. Briggs wrote with typical generosity of vision, 'I wanted my history to be definitive in that it was to be authoritative'[12] but he never saw them as inhibiting or exclusionary: on the contrary he saw them as the beginning of work for others rather than the end of it. They were to be 'a' history of broadcasting rather than 'the' history. Footnotes and quotations from original sources were particularly extensive because he saw the work as opening up the material for later historians. In fact, some of the best 'official' histories of the war were really written out of a commitment to contemporary reform and with an active engagement with future development rather than producing an ideological version of the past. In many ways it is this engaged tradition that Briggs developed, but his commitment was to the priceless quality and contribution of popular culture when made with integrity.

In between thinking up Sussex University's influential reconstruction of knowledge (now abandoned) and making it a new university that for a blissful moment threw all the grim social and intellectual hierarchies of British life into disarray (simply because it was the most exciting, sexiest academy); being the Chancellor of the Open University at a formative moment and then running Worcester College Oxford (and much, much, more – the Arts Council, the British Council, lots of historical organisations, being on the boards of museums), Briggs produced five stunning volumes of BBC history.[13] Because he had run institutions he understood how large organisations work – and this brought an almost Dickensian width and grasp to the work. They vary in focus, but each is an Aladdin's cave crammed with insight and a calm, wise breadth of vision. The detail is all there, and whenever a problem arises Briggs can be relied on to have dealt with it – but there is also the broad sweep.

Briggs wrote 'I have wished to concentrate on what people had in mind at the time and how and why that changed', and he set himself the discipline of 'never looking round corners' to what they, then, could not see. His volumes offer a panorama of a great institution adapting, occasionally licking its wounds, sometimes flourishing and at others stuffy, rigid. But rather like Peter Hennessy's work on civil servants later, there is also a sense of bringing out into the open a shy and often sequestered but honourable beast: the British administrator. Who, it turns out, is often a passionate and competent animal, full of life, argument, tenacity and dogged dedication to ideals. Briggs' portrait of John Reith, the towering Presbyterian and puritanical creator of the BBC, is better than any of the biographies of the first Director General. Reith, Briggs observed, 'told me that if I had written to ask for his help on BBC notepaper he would have thrown the letter into the wastepaper basket',[14] (and one notes that few BBC Director Generals leave the Corporation happy men – probably because it is such a wonderful opportunity yet such a political job).

Reith at home was a difficult, perpetually dissatisfied man, the ancient mariner of broadcasting – 'Another wasted Sunday afternoon,' he writes typically in his diary, 'futile, miserable waste of time. It rains and I do not like lunch, I row with Muriel, and the children are unable to play decently. Despicable.'[15] But Briggs' Reith is another kind of man altogether – and the one that matters: shrewd, energetic, domineering but imaginative with an acute eye for business and political opportunity, a driven man but a fearless operator. Reith was not miserable at all when he was making decisions and getting them implemented, when he was fighting governments and business in order to make something superior for the British public. Briggs has a tremendous sense for the telling character, the clever, wry, stubborn and at times downright insubordinate memo, combined with a genuine understanding of engineering and technology and its vital importance, and an ear sensitive to men and women trying to make programmes that people like and that also – not in a preachy way (well only occasionally in a preachy way) – do them good.

Indeed, many of the best histories of institutions have been written by people who have also written biographies: John Grigg on *The Times* and Lloyd George, Philip Zeigler on Barings and Mountbatten, Kathy Burk on A.J.P. Taylor and Deutsche Bank.[16] Catching the nuances and character of the institution that endure over time is a matter not just of detail, but of the life of the place as a whole. Briggs is part of this tradition – but he also brought a sensitivity for the period. The BBC has always had a strong sense of itself and a coherent character – people have felt that working for it was special and that it entails a duty to ideals – even if they often think that the place is letting them down, betraying the ideals, going to the dogs.

Since Briggs, there have been many histories of broadcasting. Paddy Scannell and David Cardiff's *A Social History of British Broadcasting* looked at broadcasting as a tremendously creative social machine, which in seeking to represent British society, ordinary people talking in their own voices, simultaneously produced communities, and was the most brilliant of these. Humphrey Carpenter has mined the BBC in various ways, from his outstanding work on music from the biography of Benjamin Britten, to the history of the Third Programme, as well as a sensitive account of Dennis Potter and the Satire boom of the Sixties.[17] These marvellous books have all attempted to relate individual creativity to institutional opportunities. Many of these have explored aspects of the programming – case studies in cultural history. They have perhaps seen broadcasting as a way into the history of the times. There have also been some wonderful novels – Penelope Fitzgerald's *Human Voices*, for example, is a gem.

\* \* \*

A central problem is creativity – how does good broadcasting get made? By giving imaginative people with an ear for the mood of the times enough space to make something that people then recognise. Yet, quite often in broadcasting the source of creativity is also at an organisational level. Would the Sixties satire boom, TW3, and the fresh air of young ideas that swept through broadcasting have taken off without a Director General in Hugh Greene with direct experience in pre-war Germany of the biting power of cabaret? Greene wanted programmes like that and got them. In doing so the Corporation caught the mood of the times – and like all great art forms opened a discussion with those that consumed it. How did Dennis Potter's path-breaking dramas get made? *Pennies from Heaven, The Singing Detective* – they all needed organisational confidence and support – not least because they broke many of the prevailing rules about how things should be done, as well as what audiences would accept. In a different way the creation of a ground-breaking documentary series or a successful soap opera is usually seen as a consequence of the creative decisions that the writers and producers made and this is, of course, essential. But who chose the writer and the producer?

Who identified the need in the schedules or the place that would allow them to flourish? Who found the considerable resources for setting up a long-running show? Who gave the writers and directors and producers the space to do what they wanted? These decisions are often taken by people far higher up in broadcasting organisations and are in part a product of the organisation's sense of what its priorities should be.

Yet sometimes other pressures set programmes going – for example, technological change. News, outside broadcasts, the style of drama are all driven by what cameras, microphones and transmitters can do. Recently there has been an argument about how compromised 'embedded' reporters were in the war in Iraq. But this is just another staging-post in a long-running debate between soldiers, journalists and what the contemporary technology permits near battlefields. Soldiers used to like to keep journalists at a safe distance and out of their way; now they like to keep the journalists at a safe distance – and take them with them. Many journalists feel that they spend too much time reporting and too little finding out what has happened – but this is because the technology developed to feed twenty-four-hour news can take them to battlefields in a novel way – yet once they are there, requires a constant diet of stories, like a hungry monster. Technological innovation drives more in broadcasting than is usually recognised. People seek to exploit what is available.

Then there are the people. Broadcasting has over the last seventy years simply called on some of the cleverest, wittiest, most creative and ambitious individuals, supported by legions of wily administrators. They loved the work – talking to people employed in the BBC or Channel 4 in the 1980s, it is clear that despite the rows, they all thought that what they were doing was worthwhile – that it mattered. So you do broadcasting history just like any other kind, by talking with individuals and getting groups together. In a history as heated as the BBC everyone has a story. One of the groups we have talked to about the 1980s is that of the men (and unusually for the BBC, it was all men) who sorted the money, dealt with the unions, dealt with the engineering. They were back-room boys. They told us very good stories about managing money in a tough climate, and the ways in which they had to change the whole culture of the Corporation. But beyond what they told us was the clear evidence of a committed, intelligent team of principled administrators who worked together with a clear idea of purpose. Of course top mandarins have their stories to tell, and they tell them cogently. All of the great ones have also been showmen – they had to deliver services that worked. The men and women who ran broadcasting were carnivores. But there are other levels of people to talk to in broadcasting.

It is always worth talking to cameramen. They are observers and often not directly engaged in whatever interaction is taking place – but they often see and understand a great deal of what is happening. Secretaries know a thing or two as well. Interviews animate the files, explain the real story and give you a flavour of the people and their concerns.

It's the programmes, stupid. Of course writing broadcasting history is ultimately about programmes. It is about how broadcasters have a discussion with audiences. How they conceive of audiences, and how they put together programmes that we see ourselves reflected in and informed by. It is about the exuberant creativity that makes programmes work. But how should one deal with the programmes? When Asa Briggs was asked to write the first volume of the history of the BBC he could see the files and he could interview the people, both of which he did with a consummate mastery – but he could not (and the technology did not permit him to) watch the programmes again or listen to the tapes. Most programmes were not saved. So although he knew that the programmes were central to what it was the BBC did, and although he writes with sensitivity and verve about why some programmes worked and others offended or caused problems, he did not have to confront them again himself. This is no longer the case – and anyone writing about the history of programmes has to deal with what programmes made then, felt like then. Making the programmes central to the history is a challenge, not least because there are so many of them. During the 1980s, the period I am concerned with, the BBC broadcast on two television stations and three radio stations, as well as the World Service, local radio and the Open University. It would take more than several decades to watch and listen to the product of a decade. So, while it is important, how can one do it? And then how does one use what one sees or hears – how does it fit together with what is in the files, and what people tell you?

Well, there is, as it turns out, one unexpected advantage in age – the TV one has watched and the radio one has listened to – in the past. During most of the 1980s I was surrounded by an increasing tribe of small boys. So I watched – for example – more breakfast television with grumpy wakeful babies than before or since. Of course what I watched was heavily biased; I did not do it then as a researcher but just as a person. I watched lots of news, *Newsnights*, *Panoramas* and *World in Actions*, every single *Yes Minister*, *Blackadder*, Attenborough on animals, *Not the Nine O' Clock News*, plays, drama, *Tumbledown* and epics on Queens, *Morse*, *Miss Marple* and *A Very British Coup*, everything by Dennis Potter, starting with *The Blue Remembered Hills*. I watched Mrs Thatcher mutate from frump into Byzantine empress. I watched Charles and Diana kissing (accompanied by an eighteen-stone Rousseau-reading Republican crane driver from Redcar who was staying with us – and who wept at the key moment). Also, as the decade wore on, a good deal of *Blue Peter*. I got other people up, cooked, had baths and drove cars to Radios Three and Four with enormous – slightly clandestine – private pleasure. We drank our coffee and went to school and work to the *Today* programme. My best friend and I sat in Oxford and watched the British fleet sail to the Falklands and felt a chill flutter of anxiety as we both held our newborn sons on our knees and watched war coming. I dealt with coming home from work to toddlers with a cup of tea, and *Playbox*. Later homework would start as *Neighbours* and *The Simpsons* ended. I had christenings where all the small children in sight had plastic swords down the back of their jumpers – a strange accessory – but one directly derived from a cartoon called *Thunderbirds*.

But I glanced at or rejected a good deal more. So one answer is a broad view of shows that worked (at least for us) and also some feeling for those one did not watch as well, a kind of map. Not a method but a feeling – and a Geiger counter of where to start to look again. If one wants to see whether the dry economic revolution that stimulated Thatcherism was facilitated or impeded by broadcasting I at least know you start to look at *The Money Programme*, listen to *Analysis*, and look at the files on *Moneybox*. Looking back at a decade's viewing and listening in a broader way, also provides some sense of where broadcasting fitted into my own, admittedly privileged, life. The way television and radio shape and accommodate social change. The way we use television to baby-sit children, and as a family recourse after Sunday supper. A feeling of the shape of the thing as it meshes with experience, and the unexpected shifts of history. This, it seems to me, is also part of writing about the history of broadcasting – because it reflects such alterations with a dazzling immediacy.

So you look at programmes that caused rows, great programmes, programmes that illustrate themes, and try and sample the flow of things. But none of this is quite systematic, and I do not think it can be. But what do you do with what you make of programmes when you see them again? You see how broadcasting makes arguments, how styles develop, how it addresses audiences. Any past broadcast is located in the conventions of its moment – and they all seem different from contemporary habits. Fixing what was innovation and what was a convention is part of what is to be established. But you also see the programmes through what there is in the files, and then you also have to see the files and the programmes in the light of what people tell you. Sometimes the files send you to the programmes and sometimes the programmes send you to the files. The files have a whole world of thought and argument and direction which illuminate something of how people were thinking. Programmes are like icebergs – what you see is a fraction of the work that goes into making them, and sometimes that thought is more important than the programmes themselves. There is one priceless guide – the BBC's programme review meetings. Here on a weekly basis across the whole range of output people of intelligent engagement in programmes discussed frankly what worked and what did not work, what did its job in the schedules and why. There is the tantalising whiff of the scent of the times, what people worried about and enjoyed. So this is a prompt of the highest kind.

One aspect of considering programming is scheduling, the ways in which putting together the stream of programmes that will call, attract and hold audiences over an evening, a week, a year is thought of. So sometimes programmes are just bits of a jigsaw, what will catch viewers and listeners in that mood at that time of day. For broadcasters scheduling is an enormously emotionally charged and intellectually demanding issue – as they juggle importance, what the competition is putting on, time of day and audience suitability. At others all you can do (and it's the best you can do) is to makes sense of some of the programmes as collective or individual creations. Great series take years of preparation and investment. Drama that catches a mood or stirs a reaction or game shows that people like, all have to be planned and fought over. Partly because some programmes are in themselves important they change things, they set new benchmarks, they are good or bad or of the moment. Yet because broadcasting is one of the last craft industries, despite the creep (and comfort) of formats, broadcasting has always had to make individual programmes – and it is to the creative dialogue such programmes set going, with ever changing audiences, that scheduling shapes.

\* \* \*

Ideally, writing broadcasting history at times brings all of these different levels together. It does so most clearly over the *cause célèbre* programmes – those that become the great set-pieces of folklore and precedent. Then for a moment you can glimpse policy and market pressures, institutional thinking and process grinding their wheels beside people making editorial choices and putting programmes together. But you can see it too – less distinctly – in how the run of material gets commissioned and put together. You can see it all in some very distinct practises – public service broadcasting, the state of competition, government policy and the mood of the institution, the rigour of principals and the necessity of expediency will all be pressures that you can see worked out in a single decision to cut a picture, edit a story in a very particular way. Much great broadcasting has come from leaving people alone to come up with something – and then giving the programme enough air to grow an audience. (Something which is less and less possible in the contemporary harsh commercial climate, where series are given one swift chance in the ratings war.) There are intriguing problems; sometimes political and commercial threats seem to have little influence on creativity – at others calm waters do better. But broadcasters are articulate complainers and sensitive of their rights. At other times you do the work of the whole better by looking at the illuminating detail of putting one programme together.

Yet in the end, the issue is an unfashionable, old-fashioned one of institutions. Broadcasting makes history – but it makes it out of traditions and constraints and by simultaneously hunting down public taste and forming it. If broadcasting does it well then individual creativity thrives and our lives – as citizens and as people who just want something to watch after work – are genuinely enriched. We lose a great deal if it does it badly. How you grow great institutions, secure and adaptable yet looking after us – caring for our societies – is one of the great mysteries of contemporary history. Writing the history of broadcasting shows us how it has been done in the past and warns us about what needs preserving. It is after all easy to destroy institutions – and far harder to build them well.

## Notes

\* This work was supported by the AHRB.
1. See Joshua Meyorwitz, *No Sense of Place. The Impact of the Electronic Media on Social Behaviour*, Oxford, Oxford University Press, 1985.
2. See Stephanie Marriot, 'Elections as Media Events' in *Media, Culture and Society*, vol. 27, no. 3, 2002.
3. Brian Hanrahan, at a BBC seminar at the beginning of the war on Afghanistan 2001.
4. Paddy Scannell has elaborated this kind of insight in a series of works of great originality, see Paddy Scannell and David Cardiff, *A Social History of British Broadcasting*, Oxford, Blackwell, 1991, and Paddy Scannell, *Radio, Television and Modern Life*, Oxford, Blackwell, 1996. Humphrey Carpenter's work has been focused on creativity and he understands the unique power of broadcasting in the formation of musical repertoires and audiences better than anyone else.

David Hendy's forthcoming work on the *History of Radio Four* deals with the ways programmes are made as part – evidently of both speaking to and representing – 'middle England'. His careful, sensitive work shows how class, culture, taste and power are brokered in programmes.

5. Interview with Ron Neil.
6. Richard Sennet, *The Fall of Public Man*, London, Faber & Faber, 1993.
7. See Michael Scudsen, the outstanding American historian of the media, in *The Power of the News*, New York, Columbia University Press, 1999, or *The Good Citizen*, London, Harvard University Press, 2000.
8. Asa Briggs, Collected Essays, vol. 1 *Words Numbers Places People*, London, Harvester Press, 1985, p. 113.
9. See Independent Televison Commission Annual Report 2003.
10. Asa Briggs, 'Problems and Possibilities in the Writing of Broadcasting History', *Media Culture and Society*, 1980, p. 5.
11. See Steve Barnett, *British Journalism Review*, April, 2003, p. 23.
12. Asa Briggs, *Governing the BBC*, was an offshoot of the histories and yet has been a kind of operational bible within the Corporation – heavily thumbed in any crisis.
13. Asa Briggs, *The History of Broadcasting in the United Kingdom*: Vol. I *The Birth of Broadcasting*, 1961; Vol II *The Golden Age of Wireless*, 1965; Vol III *The War of Words*, 1970; Vol IV *Sound and Vision*, 1979; Vol V *Competition*, 1995; Oxford, Oxford University Press.
14. Asa Briggs 'Problems and Possibilities', p. 2.
15. Charles Stuart (ed.), *The Reith Diaries*, London, Collins, 1930, p. 157.
16. For example: John Grigg, *The History of The Times*, Vol. 6 *The Thomson Years, 1966–81*, London, Times Books, 1993; John Grigg, *Lloyd George: War Leader 1916–18*, London, Penguin, 2003; Phillip Ziegler, *Mountbatten*, London, Collins, 1985; Phillip Ziegler, *The Sixth Great Power: Barings 1762–1929*, London, Collins, 1988; Kathy Burk, *Die Deutsche Bank in London 1873–1998*, Munchen, Piper, 1998; Kathy Burk, *Troublemaker: The Life and History of A.J.P. Taylor*, New Haven/London, Yale University Press, 2000.
17. Paddy Scannell and David Cardiff, *A Social History of British Broadcasting*, Oxford, Blackwell, 1991; Paddy Scannell, *Radio, Television and Modern Life*, Oxford, Blackwell, 1996; Humphrey Carpenter, *The Envy of the World: Fifty Years of the BBC Third Programme*, London, Weidenfeld and Nicolson, 1996; Humphrey Carpenter, *Dennis Potter*, London, Faber & Faber, 1998.

# 11
## Has Hollywood Stolen Our History?

*David Puttnam*

In recent years, it has become almost commonplace to claim that Hollywood has stolen our history. Newspapers in the UK for example regularly carry stories reporting on the latest Hollywood blockbuster and how it has traduced some episode of British military daring, invariably by substituting American heroes for the British originals. But Hollywood has not so much 'stolen' our history as 'simplified' it; and this simplification has had a corrosive effect on the whole culture of contemporary film-making. The best way to explain the impact of this simplification is by returning to my own origins, and examining the way in which I originally fell in love with cinema.

*     *     *

I have always adored the movies, ever since as a small boy I became a regular visitor to my local cinema, just one of five within easy walking distance of my home. The first film I ever saw was *Pinocchio*, to which I was taken by an aunt. I still remember how it felt coming out of that film. The words of the song 'When You Wish Upon a Star' ringing in my ears. I distinctly remember thinking; 'I want to make people feel exactly like I feel now.' Interestingly, the lyrics of that song continue to represent the idea that drove cinema almost from its beginning. The audience is invited to join in with the dreams being acted out on that vast screen. We are given the opportunity to leave our individual troubles behind, and in darkness to borrow the pleasures and pains, loves and losses, laughter and tears, or triumphs or disasters, of others. That's what I have always believed film should offer – even if I'm no longer convinced that film-makers fully understand that particular collective dream.

It was at the movies that I acquired much of my early sense of what was interesting about life. As a boy I would sit in the cinema and absorb the lessons of films like Fred Zinneman's *The Search*, William Wyler's *Best Years of Our Lives*, Elia Kazan's *East of Eden* or, a little later, Stanley Kramer's *Inherit the Wind*. Many of these films were somewhat critical of America, but they also demonstrated that 'pursuit of happiness' that is so uniquely enshrined in the American constitution. The way that Stanley Kramer's *Inherit the Wind* deals with historical events is a fine example of this. The film, the story of the 'Scopes/Monkey trial', concerns itself with the right of a teacher to discuss, in the early 1920s, in his own classroom, Darwin's Theory of Evolution, in opposition to what was then, at least in Kansas, the accepted community belief.

In a very moving courtroom scene, the somewhat cynical lawyer Clarence Darrow (played by Spencer Tracy) is confronted by the presidential candidate William Jennings Byran who demands of Darrow whether he believes in *anything* that's sacred. Darrow retorts emphatically 'Yes!', and continues by saying:

I believe in the individual mind. In a child's power to master the multiplication table there is more sanctity than in all of your shouted 'Amens!' An idea, is a greater monument than a cathedral ... Why did God plague us with the power to think? Why do you deny the one faculty which lifts man above all other creatures on earth; the power of his brain to reason?

*Inherit the Wind* concerns itself with the value of the individual, and the right to think and express oneself even in opposition to all received wisdom. It offers a vision, one that reminds us that a just society has to be built around beliefs which bind its members together, beliefs which are themselves built on that pursuit of happiness, liberty, justice and truth. Just as importantly, it provides its audience with an understanding of a historical debate which had, and continues to have, huge social, moral and cultural consequences. It is a film that offers us what every film should aspire to; it offers dreams, knowledge and understanding.

\* \* \*

The vast majority of films cranked out by the Hollywood studios today have no such similar ambition. Unfortunately 'Hollywood' effectively dominates the world's cinema screens – while itself remaining dominated by the tyranny of the so-called 'bottom line'. Dreams, maybe, but knowledge, understanding, the advancement of what it means to be a complex human being – these issues seldom even enter the equation. We are all aware that Hollywood has never suffered the least embarrassment in taking dramatic liberties with historical truth. Sometimes, as I can attest from my own experience, a degree of licence can be justified as a means of engaging the audience, sometimes as a way of offering even greater insight into the motivation of this or that character.

Hollywood's refusal to engage with complexity is symptomatic of the way in which much of contemporary cinema has ceased to exploit the real potential of the medium; most especially in respect of history. In my book *The Undeclared War* (1997),[1] I argued that it was because film is such an extraordinary medium for conveying ideas, and shaping our sense of who we are, that its power was recognised so very early on by all manner of politicians. It was Lenin who said , 'Of all the arts, for us cinema is the most important.' Other political leaders, including Winston Churchill, recognised how powerfully film could change the way we see the world. Former President Woodrow Wilson called film 'The very highest medium for the dissemination of public intelligence.' He added that 'since it speaks a universal language, it lends itself importantly to the presentation of America's plans and America's purposes'.[2]

Cinema should have remained a medium of enormous significance to today's global society – especially during uncertain times such as those we are living through. But too often over the past twenty-odd years filmmakers have failed to tap the emotional power of their medium; especially its ability to portray the world around us – either as it is, or as it has been. But for the most part it fails to offer us any useful lessons. After September 11, any number of writers noted that the dreadful images witnessed that day seemed to have more in common with a contemporary movie than any imagined reality. But somehow even this description felt inadequate, and not just because of the scale of the tragedy itself.

That 'catastrophe' should have woken Hollywood up, because for too long cinema had been playing games with reality, as well as with history. It had been playing with them by allowing actions to become entirely divorced from their consequences; ever bigger explosions that miraculously don't kill the most important of the characters; simulated plane crashes which the right people 'somehow' survive; shootings that somehow manage to create victims, without widows or orphans. Having watched the details of a brutal homicide, in how many movies do we then see a policeman walk up a garden path to tell a woman that her husband is dead? And then witness that mother having to decide whether to tell her twelve-year-old child, who is about to appear in the school play, that her father has been killed?

This is the stuff of real human history; these are the consequences of tragic actions. Yet, with a few notable exceptions, here is a whole world of human experience that has effectively been abandoned, or left to the comparative simplicities of the small-screen 'soap opera'. It is in this sense that we can legitimately claim that contemporary film-making has extracted very little of value from history. It merely reduces events, now or in the past, to a simple struggle between good and evil; a struggle in which complexity and nuance have been entirely wrung out of the narrative. It's not that history has been 'stolen', it's been subject to a grossly simplistic reduction. It's as if the movies have returned to their very earliest days – before they grew up – when all the audience demanded was the thrill of standing in front of that 'Lumière Brothers' train as it seemed about to run them over! It's almost as if the movies had never left the fairground.

The reality should have been far more interesting. More than a hundred years after that first train appeared on the screen, cinema should have established itself as possibly the most powerful and effective means of communication with which we have ever been able to express ourselves. We refer to Hollywood as 'Tinseltown' as if it didn't really matter. Some people try to persuade us that films and television are a business just like any other. They are not. Films and television (like newspapers) shape attitudes and behaviour, and in doing so, reinforce or undermine many of the wider values of society. We have come to accept that cinema's influence on people's behaviour, and their sense of history, is a global phenomenon. We should recognise, for instance, that thousands or even millions of young people are growing up in incredibly distressed circumstances. Wherever they are concentrated in the world – every one of these locations is a 'tinderbox' which could explode at any moment. It's important that we reflect on the fact that simplistic and insensitive plots, images and stereotypes can only make those explosions that much more inevitable.

\* \* \*

Somehow we have to develop the ability to understand what powerlessness and the loss of freedom feel like as an 'everyday reality' – and what they inevitably lead to. Sadly, I don't sense that the overwhelming majority of films are in any way helping us achieve that understanding. A couple of years ago I came across a study by scientists from Israel's

Weiztmann Institute regarding a mechanism that is buried in the human visual system. This mechanism is of particular significance to film-makers. It appears that our brain is flooded with a multitude of interpretations of everyday reality. In the end, the brain must decide in favour of just one of them – and act accordingly. And from the moment the brain decides in favour of a single interpretation of the images it is receiving, then any image that supports any other interpretation of the world simply 'disappears'. The brain as it were 'edits' them out.[3] Film-makers know only too well how easy it is to paint reality this way. In the words of the remarkable Israeli writer, David Grossman,

> In the impossible relationships that exist in the Middle East, South East Asia, Northern Ireland and many other parts of the world, each competing ideology has for years appeared to suffer from almost complete blindness to reality's complexity. Each is certain that the other is not telling the truth; that the other side has no interest in peace.
>
> Each nation turns its darkest, most hateful, most bestial side to the other. Neither nation senses how deeply hatred and violence have seeped into its heart – until they quite literally wear each other out, until they have no more strength to fight. Perhaps then, a moment before their death, they will stop and do what it's already clear that they must do – compromise, try to live beside each other, and not instead of each other.[4]

This is why cinema, and its relationship with history and the 'real world', matters. The most important role of the film-maker is to help explain the ambiguities and complexities of life. And in doing so to promote understanding and, where necessary, compromise. That is what I tried to do in the films I've produced that dealt with historical events, most obviously in *The Killing Fields*, *The Mission* and *Cal*, but also, in its own way, *Chariots of Fire*. The extraordinarily complex relationship between the cultural and the commercial power of cinema, which has been argued over throughout its history, looks set to continue or even grow in importance in the decades ahead. But if film-makers simply make movies which rely on technology and special effects to portray their world, then I fear that the difference between the demands of mainstream cinema and our everyday reality could well become just too great, with consequences which will ultimately affect all of us.

I'm reminded of a story told by the outstanding French screenwriter Jean-Claude Carrière. In the early 1970s in Algeria, film-makers and doctors joined forces to make an educational documentary about an eye disease particularly virulent in that country. People were trained and sent out to screen the film in villages and organise discussions around it. The disease, a form of Trachoma, is caused by a fly and this fly was shown in close-up several times on the screen. It became all too evident from the reaction of the villagers that the film did not affect them. They even seemed somewhat surprised they had been asked to watch it. 'But almost every one of you has this disease', said an exasperated doctor. 'Yes', replied the villagers, 'but we don't have flies anything like that big here!'[5]

In a similar way, many of today's films run the risk of opening up an ever growing gap between the world of cinema and people's experience of everyday life. I believe that this reduction of history represents an opportunity for film-makers in Europe and indeed other parts of the world outside the United States. British and European film-makers are especially well-placed to reflect the complexity of our world. Unlike many in Hollywood who unquestioningly believe that they operate at the epicentre of the universe, we know from hard experience that we most certainly do not. But as a consequence of our particular history, we are, or ought to be, better placed to create sophisticated but accessible stories, stories which demonstrate a genuine empathy and understanding of the real world.

If we simply become manufacturers of films which rely on technology, special effects and emotional simplicity to portray our world, then I fear that we are storing up problems that few if any of us are equipped to address – let alone resolve. I remain hopeful that a new generation of talented film-makers will emerge with the skills and ambition to recover at least some sense of the complexity of human history. But this will depend on an ability to look beyond the personal, the expedient, 'the quickly achievable', the selfish, and embrace a vision of cinema that contains sufficient generosity of imagination to look beyond our own lives and to begin to understand the point of view of others. To empathise with them; with their sense of justice, their sense of identity, and their sense of their own history.

\* \* \*

There is a quote from the great Russian director Andrei Tarkovsky which I have been using for almost twenty years but which I still think captures all of this quite beautifully. Shortly before his death, Tarkovsky wrote this:

The connection between man's behaviour and his destiny has been destroyed; and this tragic breach is the cause of his growing sense of uncertainty in the modern world ... because he has been conditioned into the belief that nothing depends on him, and that his personal experience will not affect the future, he has arrived at the false and deadly belief that he has no part to play in the shaping of even his own fate...I am convinced that any attempt to restore harmony in the world can only rest on the renewal of personal responsibility.[6]

He was, of course, talking about film-makers.

## Notes

1. David Puttnam, *The Undeclared War: The Struggle for Control of the World's Film Industry*, London, HarperCollins, 1997.
2. Woodrow Wilson to William Brady, 28 June 1917, Series 4, File 72, Woodrow Wilson Papers (Library of Congress Microfilm) Reel 199.
3. Cited in David Grossman 'We have garrotted our own necks with a chain of violence', *Guardian*, 19 December 2001.
4. Ibid.
5. Story adapted from *The Secret Language of Film*, Jean-Claude Carrière, trans. by Jeremy Leggatt, New York, Pantheon Books, 1994, p. 51.
6. An edited version of this quote is at www.cinemaseekers.com/Tarkovsky.html.

# Index

*Compiled by Sue Carlton*